COME UP BIG

My Journey Through Vietnam, Harvard, the
White House, the Department of State, and as
CEO in Corporate America

COME UP BIG

My Journey Through Vietnam, Harvard, the White House, the Department of State, and as CEO in Corporate America

Charles W. B. Wardell III

BookGo

Copyright © 2025 by Charles W. B. Wardell III

All rights reserved. No part of this book may be reproduced in any manner whatsoever without written permission except in the case of brief quotations embodied in critical articles and reviews.

All photos in this book are the property of the author, Charles W.B. Wardell III. Any use or copying of the images without the written permission of the author is prohibited.

All inquiries should be addressed to BookGo at www.bookgo.pub

Cover Design by Khadijah Ali
Front Cover Photo Oliver F. Atkins, White House Photographer
Back Cover Image M. Cole Chilton

First Printing, 2025

This book is a memoir of my life so far. I have tried to recreate events, locales, and conversations from my memories of them, and whenever possible, offer photographic evidence in support of events which even I still find improbable: feats of luck, or hard work, or the acts of good people. Some of the conversations were recreated and/or supplemented, and also the details of some individuals have been changed to respect their privacy. Please enjoy or forgive, as you see fit. With my thanks,
Chuck Wardell

I happily dedicate this book to all those who have ever been counted out—the counters suck, so stay the course.

Chuck Wardell

"Experience is a hard teacher because she gives the test first, the lesson afterward."
Vern Law, Pitcher, Pittsburgh Pirates
(1950-51, 1954-67)

TABLE OF CONTENTS

Preface

Chapter 1: "If you pass the helicopter test, you get a helicopter."

Chapter 2: "He come up big."

Chapter 3: "Everyone has his turn in the barrel."

Chapter 4: "Sleeping sentries get you killed."

Chapter 5: "The miracle bounce."

Chapter 6: "Access without authority."

Chapter 7: "Steaming down the hallway with hot news."

Chapter 8: "Never turn down a job not offered."

Chapter 9: "All is lost! Take to the boats!"

Chapter 10: "Praise the job gods."

Chapter 11: "Do it with the army you have."

Chapter 12: "Let my world take a look."

Acknowledgments

Index

PREFACE

The first president of the United States who I ever saw in person was Dwight Eisenhower. He was in an open car, driving to Theodore Roosevelt's old house on Sagamore Hill near Oyster Bay, New York on the north shore of Long Island where I grew up. It was June 14, 1953, and I was eight years old, standing by the roadside with my father, waving an American flag at the president as he drove past. Little did I know on that day that my future would have me working in the White House for two presidents. All that I knew then was that I saw the leader of my country in person. He was a real hero in battle and in politics, and I was thrilled.

President Eisenhower was making this trip in order to dedicate Theodore Roosevelt's house as a national shrine. I was not at the dedication, but I have read the speech that Eisenhower gave in which he spoke about Roosevelt's extraordinary leadership. "We look up and study the actions of leaders, to see what were the problems facing them; how did they analyze them; how did they reach their decisions; what did they do," Eisenhower told the gathered. "One of the men who was a favorite for study in my generation was Theodore Roosevelt."

Eisenhower went on to explain that, in Roosevelt, he saw "a man who understood his fellow human beings. He understood those things for which they yearned and which they deserved under the principles in which he believed." He praised Roosevelt some more and, at the end of his speech, he offered a prescription: "If each of us could dedicate himself to attempt to emulate Theodore

Roosevelt in his consideration for what we so futilely call 'the common man' for want of a better word—that if we could emulate the devotion of that American citizen to all citizens, if we could have his courage in carrying through, his wisdom in seeing what was right and adhering to the right, then I am quite certain that not only will Sagamore Hill and this house stand as a great monument, but each of us in his own way will build a little monument to America."

Eisenhower had been part of what author and journalist Tom Brokaw called the "greatest generation" of Americans, those who took up the cause of liberty and justice with the willingness to sacrifice their lives in the name of it as they fought the Nazis and the fascist peril in Europe and the Pacific. He was part of that generation who made today's world, even with all its problems and challenges, possible.

I served in the military, as well, spending a year in quite a bit of combat in the jungles of Vietnam. I also served two presidents, Nixon and Ford, while I worked in the White House, and throughout the course of my long life I have had the honor to meet nine presidents. These events would have certainly surprised—and probably scared the wits out of—my eight-year-old self, waving at President Eisenhower on that warm June day in 1953.

I have been graced by an interesting life, which has also been a great surprise because there were a couple of times when I didn't think an interesting life, or any kind of life at all, would happen for me.

On my journey in this life, I have seen and learned

a lot. My purpose in writing this book is to share my story with those who were also counted out, so you might find a way to count yourself in. That said, this isn't only a book about being counted out and finding a way to be counted in, but also a book about how I went about learning to become someone who was responsible for the success of others as I made my way—making more than a few mistakes—to now. It's the story of how I became me. Which is something that I never thought would happen.

I didn't start out with some grand vision bouncing around in my head. Honestly, my primary quest in life was to get a job and just to be employable. I had no notion of becoming any kind of leader when I began my journey even though I did become one, many times over, on many different fronts.

At first in my life there was no leadership: I was dyslexic, I could not read and could not spell and so I had a tough time trying to make the grade in school. But I kept going and then a leader stepped up when a teacher took action on my behalf. I was given direction and valued, and I gladly accepted it. And on it went, from my time in sports to my time in the academic world to combat in the military to service in the White House and the Department of State and to the billion-dollar world of corporate life as a CEO. I rose rank by rank and job by job, rising to the level at which good leadership was asked of me and which was also supported in me, until I became a leader myself.

So, my journey in this book is not one of judgment, but of perspective, and not one of self-congratulation but of amazement. It's my view of what I saw and heard and did. The history I explore is my own because I am not an academic historian. However, that said, my story—quite a lot of it, actually—clearly intersects with American history.

It was at the White House that I first understood what a presidential decision means. General Alexander Haig, the Chief of Staff to President Richard Nixon, used to say, "A president makes four major decisions a year. And they are big ones." I have made decisions, too—and, while they are nowhere as big as those a president must make, they all changed my life in profound ways, and I will tell you about them as we go. Ultimately, I know that I began my journey as part of the "wall sitter's union," which is an expression I also learned while working in the White House. It refers to the aides who sit at the edge of the room in chairs lined against the wall in those big meetings with the principal whom they serve sitting at the Big Table. Which is another way of saying that, while I got into the room, I never had a real place at that table where decisions were made.

Although I got to watch and listen and learn, I did not land at the Big Table until I became a CEO myself, and then I had to deal with boards that required me to explain why I had made the decisions that I made. And to see if I could make them listen or, better yet, agree with my decisions. They were not always readily agreeable, to put it mildly.

My perspective on my life has given me pause to reflect, which is what drives my journey to seek out those qualities that reveal the best and, sometimes, the worst in us. In telling my story, we will see what I was thinking when I made my decisions and what other people were thinking of me and how the clash of the two, even within me as I wrestled with my own conscience and even counted myself out. I forged my journey that was not always easy—but usually surprising.

So, I invite you to come with me on my journey through my life and, along the way, explore what I have been lucky to see up close: the good, and the not so good, and what we can learn from these points to make our country, our world, and ourselves better.

Chapter 1
"If you pass the helicopter test, you get a helicopter."

It was June of 1973, and I was 32,000 feet above the United States on Air Force One, thinking of an expression I had learned in the Army about how you get a helicopter. You get a helicopter by passing the helicopter test. What this expression means is that, if you train and then pass a certain test on helicopter proficiency, you'll be a licensed pilot and get to fly choppers. I needed to pass that test because I needed a job.

I was up there in the sky and heading west—not on a helicopter and not exactly on Air Force One, either—because President Richard Nixon was not on the jet, and only when the president is on board does it become Air Force One. In fact, I was the only passenger (I think, although David Hoopes, special assistant to the president whom I would get to know better later, and his family might have snuck on at the tail end) because I was on my way to San Clemente, California to see President Nixon's Chief of Staff General Alexander Haig at the "Western White House." I was going to San Clemente for a job interview.

I had recently graduated *cum laude* from Harvard College, which is itself a highly unlikely story I will get into later, and a Harvard friend had connected me to General Haig. My friend thought I might be of some use to the new chief of staff, and so I was flying west to see if the general agreed.

I was aboard Air Force One because Leonid Brezhnev, the leader of the USSR, had flown back to Washington on the president's jet after meeting with Nixon in California. The jet was returning to the Marine Corps Air Station in El Toro, California (today known as Lake Forest), and they offered me a ride. I flew down to Washington from Boston, and a White House limousine drove me to Andrews Air Force Base, and I boarded the president's plane.

As I flew over the country, staring out the window of Special Air Mission 27000, as it was known when not carrying the president, I was thinking that I was about to enter a world that I could only have dreamt of once upon a time—or would have been awestruck by—as I was when I waved a flag by the side of the road as a boy. As you will see, that dream was an awfully big one. I had also experienced a pretty turbulent route to get on this jet, in the First Lady's section, no less, and I marveled at how this had come to be. The Air Force steward asked me if I would like something to eat, and so I ordered a sandwich. The steward brought it to my seat before telling me the cost: "That will be $1.68, please." I was not a member of the White House mess, and there was no free lunch on this Air Force jet. So, I paid for my lunch and ate it, thinking that maybe the next time I was on this plane, if that day ever came, I would not have to pay for my lunch because I would be part of the team.

I landed at El Toro, the Marine base. A Marine driver met me and drove me to the San Clemente Inn. I was about to begin a new chapter in my life. I would be introduced to the White House leadership during the time of Watergate and later to the Department of State as the Assistant Deputy Secretary of State where I was dispatched around the world on State Department business. This eventually led to my work for major American companies and, eventually, as a chairman and CEO myself. Of course, I had no idea of that then. And I would not have even dared to imagine it.

I took a deep breath and looked down at the great landscape passing beneath me. I thought, if it worked, I would have an opportunity to serve my country again. Then I asked myself: how the hell did I get here?

Well, it all began in June of 1965 when I was asked to leave college after my sophomore year. 1965 was a significant year. In Selma, Alabama, Martin Luther King Jr. led Civil Rights demonstrators on a historic march pushing the passage of the Voting Rights Act, and *The Sound of Music* had just come out in the movie theaters and *Help!* by the Beatles on our radios.

Help is what I needed as I believed my life was a failure and my career prospects were greatly diminished. I would never be able to just "get by." As things would turn out, I would do more than just get by, which I am so grateful for—and still shocked by. In fact it was much more than I could ever have imagined.

Chapter 2
"He come up big."

I have had an interesting life, which was fueled by extraordinary times and driven by the mysterious gifts of dyslexia—which at first had me counted out, then later helped me count myself in as a respected leader in a war zone and later as a CEO. My story spans nearly half of the past century and continues with considerable steam into the current one. I am telling this tale because I was involved in some of the major historic incidents of the twentieth century, much to my surprise. Along the way, I learned some things about myself and about expectations and dreams, about leadership and friendship, about being counted out and counting yourself in, and about how things work in America: then and now.

Back in June 1965, I could not imagine the life that I would live because I was being asked to leave Hamilton College. When Dean Tolls called me into Hamilton's Root Hall and sourly intoned, "The weed of neglect grows bitter fruit; a strong letter to follow," which it did, my life was suddenly at a dead standstill. I was twenty years old and now asked to leave a college where I had tried my best, and my best had not been good enough. My world of academic life, social life, and sporting life all came crashing down at once. Let me tell you how this came to be.

Sports have always been important to me and, while I love to sail boats and I was a pretty good hockey player, the way I see the arc of my life is in terms of a big football game. I am standing on my own one-yard line with seconds left on the clock, and we are losing the game. Instead of throwing a Hail Mary pass, I call a quarterback sneak and make it all the way down the field and across the other team's goal line to get us the win. A seemingly impossible play to pull off, but I have had that kind of life.

Never on that day when Hamilton showed me the door could I have imagined the sixty years to follow. I could not have dreamed that I would fight in the jungles of Vietnam or go to Harvard College or work for two presidents of the United States in the West Wing of the White House or serve in Henry Kissinger's State Department or survive at a very high level in some of the world's most illustrious companies and become chairman and CEO of one of them. I still have a hard time believing it, but it all begins with an ending—with my being dismissed by Hamilton.

Before I get to that starting point, I want to tell you how I began and that requires a little time travel backward.

My family has been in the United States since before it even became a country. My founding ancestor, Thomas Wardell, emigrated from Well near Alford, Lincolnshire with his brother William in 1634, and they landed in Boston in the late summer.

When the Revolution came, the Wardells took an active stand throughout the war. They wanted no part in a revolution, so did not help the revolutionaries. They wanted to keep the status quo and so promoted the Royalist cause. Edwin Salter's list of those officers and privates in Monmouth County who fought for the patriotic cause does not include a single man named Wardell and, according to the Revolutionary census of New Jersey, there were fifteen Wardell taxable heads of family living in the province. After Yorktown, much of the family fled to Canada. Those who remained moved, over time, to Brooklyn.

It was a logical move: the Wardells were grocery men and fishermen who would have used New York Harbor as transportation to other markets in New York. Looking across Lower New York Bay, Yellow Hook—as Bay Ridge, Brooklyn was called—seems to have been a natural place to relocate.

The boat basin at 69th Street in Bay Ridge was built by Jacob Wardell, who lived on 69th Street and Shore Road in 1877.

Charles Willard was a coal dealer living in Brooklyn by the end of the Civil War. In 1883, his daughter Harriet Evelyn married Winant Bennett Wardell.

After his father died, Winant Bennett Wardell's mother, Margaret Adelia Wardell, needed work. She had become the housekeeper of Winant T. Bennett. He was a bachelor and businessman, a friend and neighbor of the Wardells who lived at the foot of 69th Street in what some maps of the time call "Wardellville."

Like Charles Willard, Winant T. Bennett was a coal merchant. When he died, he had left his coal business to Margaret and Winant Bennett Wardell. However, they changed direction. Wardell's Corner on Bay Ridge Avenue and Shore Road is the likely location of the Old Homestead Inn and Elmore Wardell's grocery store. It was owned in 1894 by Margaret A. Wardell, and the innkeeper for many years was Winant Bennett Wardell.

So, the Wardells were all Brooklyn people, and Brooklyn is where my parents Charles and Elsa moved after the war, finally ending up in Cold Spring Harbor on New York's Long Island, which is the place where I grew up.

When you think of a little East Coast town with a short Main Street, fronted by a little church with a tall spire, that's Cold Spring Harbor. In the 1950s, it was such a small hamlet that the census didn't even report the population size.

My father's family were not rich by any means, but they believed in education, and so my father Charles W.B. Wardell Junior went to Princeton, where he majored in political science and was a member of Tiger Inn, Princeton's third oldest dining society. He lettered in football for all three years that he played, and he played on the undefeated 1933 team. He also lettered in lacrosse for three years and was a first-team All-American selection in 1934 and 1935. He was captain of the undefeated 1935 team, scoring five goals against both Harvard and Yale.

During World War II, he had served his country as a lieutenant in the U.S. Navy in the Pacific. After returning from the war, he was an entrepreneur whose fortunes varied. We'd be well off and then not so well off, but he was always a man who worked hard. Let's just say I was in no way coming from a life of privilege, except when it came to how loved I was by my parents. My mother's family lived at 156 Hicks Street in Brooklyn, but it was a home plundered by loss and suicide. In 1931, my great-grandmother Ida Helen Kusenberg Meyer died, one month after her daughter Helen Julia Meyer McDonald jumped to her death in Memphis. Her son, Arnold Luther Meyer, had asphyxiated himself in his garage in Ridgewood, New Jersey, a suburb of Patterson, a year earlier.

Ida Meyer had truly done her very best to protect her granddaughter Elsa Talbot Adam from the tragic suicides and also the cruelty inflicted by the Christian Science faith of her daughter, Caroline Meyer, Elsa's mother. The nastier aspects of her mother's convictions include family stories with scenes of Caroline throwing Elsa into the freezing Hudson River with a rope tied around her to teach her how to swim or telling her that God Himself would fix her broken ankle, and that He was punishing her with the excruciating stomachache that in fact turned out to be appendicitis. She was only operated on and only survived because her sister Helen, at age fourteen, put her into a taxi to the hospital.

And so, in 1931, Elsa was a freshman at Vassar. She was hit by the awful news that she had to leave college because her bills were unpaid. She could not afford to stay and get an education—and possibly escape the challenges at home. She was preparing to come home to nothing when a dean knocked on her door and told her that her bills would be paid by a special scholarship—not only for that year, but through the rest of her time at Vassar. Fifty years later, Elsa's Vassar classmate and good friend Grace Chapman Lapham would admit that her family had written the checks to put my mother through college. It was not the last time a good friend would come to the rescue of a Wardell.

Elsa Adam and Charles W.B. Wardell Jr. met while growing up in Brooklyn and they were married in January of 1937, eventually becoming my parents.

After my mother graduated from Vassar, she worked for Henry Luce, founder of Time Inc., and she was his special assistant. She wrote a lot of Luce's material for him. In fact, she once made a note on something Luce had written that said, "This is silly!" Luce came out of his office and said, "Don't ever call me silly!" I don't know if she ever did, but I do know that she was a very smart, very progressive person, and I was very close to her.

Both my father and my mother absolutely believed that their four children came first. Proof included how my mother would never have a drink at night until dinner was finished, and we kids were bathed and in our pajamas.

My father would come to the football games I was playing in. I'd see him standing there, but he wouldn't come up to me after the game was over to congratulate me on the win or to commiserate on the loss. He had a lot of English reserve in him, and he didn't show affection. My proof of this is how I kissed him for the first time on his eightieth birthday.

However, my parents devoted their lives to their children and, as it happens, their children have devoted their lives to their children. All of us have strong children, who are all doing well, and today, they're devoting their lives to their children. So, it was a great legacy to pass on. My parents' care and concern kept me going in my early years, against an onslaught of criticism and indifference that was about to come my way.

I had an older sister, Wendy, and two younger brothers, Chris and David. In reality, my mother and father had two sets of two children. They had Wendy and then me; then, six years later, they had Chris and then David.

My mother was a smoker. It wasn't known at the time that smoking cigarettes caused premature births. She had ten miscarriages, and I was a premature baby. When I was born, I weighed a whopping two pounds. In case there is any misunderstanding about what that meant at the time, the doctor put it in harsh perspective, telling my mother, "Don't even think you've had a child because he probably won't survive."

Nevertheless, they put me in an iron lung, which is a medical device that uses pure oxygen to change air pressure around the baby's body to force its lungs to expand and contract to mimic breathing. But pure oxygen could also make babies blind. My brother Chris, who also arrived early, lost an eye because of this fact as he, too, was put in an iron lung.

Even so, the iron lung and I got along. I began to thrive, and the doctor who had given me up for dead was impressed. He said, "That kid has a will to live." He was right. And I can assure you that my will to live certainly got tested along the way.

There was a fighting spirit to go along with strong

will or a healthy sense of competition in my family, even if we didn't have a lot of money. I knew from an early age that I was a good athlete. My father had played football and lacrosse at Princeton where he was captain of the lacrosse team and also an All American. I had his athlete's genes. I loved to go sailing and, one day in the future, I would love to play golf, but my sport then was ice hockey.

Cold Spring Harbor was named for its icy cold waters, which made for some good skating ponds in the winters, so I started skating early when I was about five years old. When I was in third grade at East Woods School, they built a rink about ten minutes from our home called the Winter Club, so I could skate all the time. Skating was, to me, preferable to going to school. I hated school.

East Woods had been founded in 1946 by a group of keen parents and soon settled into a local mansion—once eyed but not purchased by the Duke and Duchess of Windsor but good enough for the East Woods School. Langdon G. Rankin was one of the early headmasters, an austere man who oversaw the expansion of the mansion and so of the student body—and also the school's bank account.

In the fourth grade, they thought that schoolwork was increasingly difficult for me and proposed that I should transfer to another school that could handle those kids who were "slow in the classroom." School was tough, and it has left scars of insecurity upon me but, even with those scars, I carried on regardless because I had no other choice. In fact, in hindsight, the lessons from the scars have taught me much more than I realized and, indeed, what in those days was my trauma has today become my strength. When you're counted out as I was, you gain more grit and determination, along with humility and a sense of humor, too, as you work to get counted in.

My fourth-grade teacher, Mr. Cardiff, stepped up for me in the face of this impending expulsion from elementary school. He told the headmaster, Mr. Rankin, that they should give me the Bellevue Wechsler IQ test before they did anything drastic like cast me adrift. Mr. Rankin, who was in no way a Mr. Chips kind of guy, nevertheless agreed, and the test was arranged. I had to leave class to take this IQ test, which, unbeknownst to me, would decide my fate at the school. I took it and, lo and behold, I got a very good score on that test.

After I came back to my fourth-grade class after my IQ test drama, Mr. Cardiff walked down the row to my desk, and he shook my hand. He said, "Young man, it's a delight to have you in my class." That meant a lot to me because that was not what I was used to hearing from teachers.

My IQ score was good enough to change Rankin's plan to have me transfer out. In fact, they told me that I had an "unbelievable IQ" compared to what they thought was going to show up on that test. They knew that I wasn't lazy and that I had a happy and stable home life, so the powers that be decided that I was just a "slow learner" despite my IQ score.

I did not know that the cause of my "slow learning" was because I had dyslexia. I did not even learn this until

I entered my junior year at the vaunted but much less supportive Taft School in Watertown, Connecticut.

Back then, my dyslexia was never connected to my academic performance by my teachers. When I was a kid in the 1950s, dyslexia meant that most people— teachers included—thought any child who had challenges with learning was just slow, AKA stupid. Dyslexia does not mean that you're stupid. It's the most common learning disability in the world, and it means that you see words, and the world, in general, differently from how people without dyslexia see things.

According to research done by the International Dyslexia Association, dyslexia affects approximately fifteen to twenty percent of the population. This means that around one out of every five people has some form of dyslexia with boys more likely than girls to be diagnosed. So, if there are eight billion people in the world, then one billion and six hundred million of us are dyslexic. That's a lot of people to count out.

It's a left brain-right brain thing. The left brain is where our spoken and written lives engage, and the right brain is the non-verbal side, dealing with space and images. Dyslexics are right brain people. Until the 1960s, dyslexia was called "word blindness." So, I had trouble spelling, reading words quickly, writing words, and "sounding out" words in my head. What might look like c-a-t to you could look like a-c-t to me.

My dyslexia didn't mean that I didn't want to learn. It just meant that I had serious challenges in getting a handle on all the academics in school when they were not adjusting to my "different" learning ability. I didn't think I was stupid. However, I also didn't know how to study or why I couldn't succeed, and why nobody was helping me, not even my parents. My family knew that I had a hard time with school but gave me a kind of stiff upper lip encouragement "to keep working at it." My parents were expressing the post-World War II mentality of pulling your socks up and getting on with things. In fact, my father's "go to" expression about what to do when encountering life's difficulties was "shake it off." As a result, school was a terribly frustrating experience for me because I was pretty much on my own, and it was hard to just shake it off.

So, I turned my hopes and dreams towards playing hockey. I was a good skater, and I had a low center of gravity, which made it hard to knock me off my skates. I played hockey at a time when players were 5'7" and 5'8", not 6'6" like they are today, so I was a normal-sized player for the time. I have good hand-eye coordination, too, which you need for hockey as the puck is small and moves fast. The other players move fast, too, and you want to have your eyes on a swivel so that you don't get stapled to the rink's boards while you're admiring the pretty pass that you just made.

I skated at left wing and at center for the East Woods School and also for the Winter Club, the skating club founded in Cold Spring in 1957 when I was in the third grade.

For high school, I was lucky to go to Taft, which is a boarding school in Connecticut which cost money, and while my parents were not rich by any means, they wanted me to get into a good school. I was also "lucky" because Taft was a hockey hotbed. Boys' hockey had been played there since Horace Taft founded the school in 1890, and it was the first school in New England to have an indoor artificial ice surface, called the "Mays Rink," which opened in 1950. I made Taft's Big Red varsity team in my junior year and played against my best friend growing up, Dwight Miller, who went to The Hotchkiss School. He was big and athletic and a very fine hockey player who would go on to play for Yale.

Indeed, after I finished my sophomore year at Taft, Dwight invited me to join his family on a trip to Europe. We sailed from New York to Liverpool and then went on to France. We had a great time riding bikes through the French countryside, eating baguettes, taking in the sun on the French Riviera, and sneaking in a bit of wine now and then.

Back at Taft, I took hockey seriously. The school had its first undefeated hockey season in 1905, and since then the school has always produced skilled and even superlative hockey players. Today, some of them even make it to the National Hockey League, like former Montreal Canadiens' captain and their first-round draft choice, Max Pacioretty, and Ryan Shannon who played for the Tampa Bay Lightning and is now the head coach of Boys Varsity Hockey at Taft.

I turned out to be a pretty good collegiate American hockey player. After Hamilton dismissed me, I was on the practice squad of the Long Island Ducks. They had a goalie, Sal Messina, who later wound up doing Rangers radio broadcasts for thirty years. Whenever a goalie made a good save, Sal would say, "He come up big." It became one of my favorite expressions. Sal Messina actually became known as Sal "Redlight" Messina because, during an exhibition game with the Rangers, he let in eight goals in one period. The red light that signaled that a goal had been scored shone a lot that night.

I followed the Rangers as a kid, and I loved the goalie Lorne "Gump" Worsley, who got his nickname because someone thought he looked like the comic strip character Andy Gump. "The Gumper," as he was also affectionately known, was the last goalie to face frozen pieces of rubber hurtling toward his head without a protective mask between the puck and his face. I loved his bravery.

My father took me to a couple of games at Madison Square Garden, which in those days was on Eighth Avenue at West 50th Street in Manhattan. I loved sitting in the dark, waiting for the Rangers to come charging out in a blaze of light, skating hard around their own end before, more often than not, going on to lose. The National Hockey League (NHL) was a six-team league until 1967, and the Rangers had some great players, including Hall of Famers Andy Bathgate, Dean Prentice, Harry Howell, Bill Gadsby—and, of course, the Gumper, who boosted the team into the playoffs for three consecutive years from 1955-58. Bathgate became the club's captain and all-time leading scorer and won the Hart Trophy as the NHL's best player in 1958-59.

Even so, other teams had better farm systems, which nurture the up-and-coming players. Montreal had a lock on all the talent in Quebec, and there was a lot of it with Maurice "The Rocket" Richard and Jean Beliveau and Boom Boom Geoffrion and dozens more. The Rangers didn't have a great talent pipeline. They only made it as far as the Stanley Cup semi-finals five of the seventeen seasons between 1950-1967. The rest of the time, they failed to qualify. Even so, they were my team, because, in the beauty of sport, there was always next year when they could turn it all around and parade the Stanley Cup in a shower of ticker tape down Broadway. Which they would eventually do in 1994, fifty years after their last Stanley Cup victory. Sometimes, next year can take a while to arrive.

    I used to listen to the hockey games at night on an old Rocket radio up in my bedroom when I was meant to be sleeping and not listening to the Rangers. And, when I was sleeping, I dreamed of hockey. It was hockey that got me into Hamilton College.

    Hamilton took me in to play hockey because Taft told them I was a great guy and that I knew my way around the ice. They said that I could handle academics. Talk about a great leap of faith.

    I had a terribly difficult journey to college and, after I was asked to leave by Hamilton, I had no idea that I would still be applying for college a few years later. I joke that, over my lifetime, I have applied to eighteen colleges, gotten into two, and gotten bounced from one. My college counselor at Taft in my senior year suggested to my father that I go to Coe, Alfred, or Monmouth, all of them small and expensive with no ivy growing on them. My father was clearly not pleased by these costly choices, and I thought they sounded like a law firm.

Even so, my grades were not good enough to get into any college. I had to go to summer school at Taft after my junior year there and academics, because of my dyslexia, were the toughest thing I faced. I was not great at math. Languages, as you might imagine, were torture. In Spanish class I had to think in Spanish and then speak it, and I was not particularly good at doing either. Let's just say I was always tense in that class, which makes it hard to learn anything. Frankly, "Chuck's a nice guy, but he's just not very bright" was the prevailing wisdom about me at Taft. Or as my friend years later, Jerry O'Brien, revised it, "not so nice, but possibly bright."

I had done what I thought were pretty good interviews at Williams College and at Middlebury, both fine, forward-thinking colleges, and both wanted me as a hockey player but, in the end, they also decided that I wouldn't be able to handle their academic workload. In fact, my senior yearbook from Taft declared that I went to Middlebury College because that's where I thought I was going to college. At the last minute, they rejected me, so I went to Hamilton instead. It's one of those ironic mementoes I carry with me. Even my high school yearbook got me wrong.

Despite all of the rejection, I was looking forward to the college that had said "yes." My best friend Dwight Miller had gone off to Yale. My father had been a Princeton man, so everyone thought I would follow, and said, "You're going to Princeton, right?" I said "No, I'm going to Hamilton."

Nobody had ever heard of Hamilton in those days as it didn't have the reputation of being a fine liberal arts college that it has today, but it was a college, and my parents took me upstate to deliver me to the academy, and it was a happy family event. My parents said that Hamilton was a great school, but I couldn't have been admitted there academically save for the fact that the head of admissions liked me. I was going to Hamilton to play hockey and had been given a scholarship for that, but I had all the aspirations and hopes that this would be a place where I would succeed on the ice and off it, as a scholar.

In September 1963, Hamilton was an all-male, private liberal arts college in Clinton, New York, which is fifty miles east of Syracuse. The school was founded in 1793 and was chartered as Hamilton College in 1812 in honor of inaugural trustee Alexander Hamilton even though he had never set foot there. They had a very good hockey team for a school its size, which was about a thousand guys.

When I went to Hamilton it was more like a sophisticated prep school in the frozen tundra of New York State. Hamilton tagged me as a "recruited hockey player," and that was good enough for them as they made no effort to help me become a successful student. It was very Victorian in its approach to academics. Either you understood the content of the classes, or you did not, but there was no institutional interest in helping me by getting a tutor to improve my academic work. It was sink or swim with no effort made by Hamilton itself to save me from drowning.

In terms of leadership it was dreadful, as Hamilton saw itself as having zero responsibility whatsoever for the students who would be calling it home for the next four years.

I decided to join a fraternity and, in the Dekes, I found friendship and fun. They were athletes who drank lots of beer and had great parties. I also had friends I had known before Hamilton who were there with me.

One of those friends is Barry Seaman who would go on to cover the White House and Washington for Time Magazine and I trust him and his memory to tell you a bit about what I was like back then.

"I had known Charlie, as I called him, from well before Hamilton. We both grew up on the North Shore of Long Island—he in Cold Spring Harbor and I in Oyster Bay," Seaman recalled.

He laughed as he remembered how he and I met. "It was while circling the dance floor at debutante parties on the North Shore of Long Island and then meeting up at the bar, and we kind of became buddies that way. And then when I found out that he was going to be going to Hamilton from Taft, as I was from Andover, I pulled together a room where I knew everybody, but they didn't know each other. One of the guys was Charlie. We ended up rooming again in our sophomore year down at the Deke house."

Barry Seaman laughed again as he recalled how he and I first made our impression on the Dekes. "In the spring of our freshman year, we were inducted into the Deke house, having been rushed by the Dekes. One of the Deke house traditions back in the day was something called the 'wine run.'

"The "wine run" was where you had to keep

running around the Deke house, and there were stations along the way where they served this absolute rotgut red wine, which we had to drink. And Charlie really got hammered, to the point where he couldn't walk very well. So we had put him into a big old wheelbarrow. We quickly wheeled Charlie all around the house, with him lying on his back in the wheelbarrow and saying, 'Let's hear it for Charlie...' And everybody would go, 'Let's hear it for Charlie!'"

Though I had been recruited to play on the hockey team, I had a standard load of college courses to manage as well. I took a geology course known as "Rocks for Jocks." I didn't understand it. I took fine arts, but I had no aptitude for it. I had to fulfill a language requirement, which as we know was difficult, and a public speaking requirement, which I actually enjoyed.

The hockey team practiced every day for two hours. We'd practice in the morning or, most often, from four to six in the afternoon. We had our own rink, but it was not particularly good. Neither was the team. I mean, the guys were fine, but our record on the ice was not so good.

Hamilton, at one point, was known for having a very good hockey team, and I guess they were trying to rebuild because, by the time I got there, we were the opposite of a very good hockey team. Nevertheless, our schedule for the season that began in October still had some powerhouses on it, and they showed us where we stood in relation to them. We lost badly to Cornell, 21-1. Ned Harkness, who went on to become head coach and then general manager of the Detroit Red Wings, was coaching them, and Ken Dryden, who went on to win six Stanley Cups with the Montreal Canadiens and five Vezina Trophies as the NHL's best goaltender, was their goalie. We had a goaltender who had never played in goal before. You can imagine by the score how far Hamilton had slid down the hockey rankings.

I remember playing against the Army with their famous coach Jack Riley who had coached the United States to Olympic hockey gold at Squaw Valley in 1960. Riley had the decency to pull their defensemen back to the red line when they were in our zone. That is, they played the minimum number of players on offense. I mean, there were little things other teams tried to do to soften the blow. Cornell and Harkness didn't do that. We had people transfer out of our hockey program to other schools because they didn't want the shame of playing at the loser hockey school, Hamilton.

Even so, when the team was losing badly, there was no finger pointing in the locker room. We all knew we were doing the best we could. We were just playing way over our heads. The coach had been at Hamilton for nearly twenty-five years, and he was a cold, monosyllabic guy. He wasn't trying to fire us up. He was just watching us get creamed, and I guess he thought that there was nothing he could do about it. He was not a leader. He didn't even teach us any new hockey plays or skills. Practices were scrimmages, so I did not learn from him how to be a better hockey player. I had been used to winning on the ice because of my own hockey skills which came naturally to me, helped along by great coaching and great teammates. Now we were just trying to avoid being totally embarrassed. However, one night, I scored three goals against Amherst, which was my only college hat trick, and probably the highlight of my Hamilton career. We won that game because of my three goals.

In addition to the hockey team where my friend Barry Seaman was one of my linemates, he reminded me we also had a football team. "In our freshman year, we had a little six-man football team that played intramural games. And Chuck was one of the ends. We had a very simple play. The quarterback would get the ball, and then the two ends would go out and split either right or left and hit one of them for seven or ten yards and keep it going down the field. And we did very well. Chuck is an excellent athlete. I remember one of his funny lines when they asked him if he ever was going to play football at Hamilton, and he said, 'I don't think they need a 150-pound slow back.' He has a great sense of self-deprecation."

Despite my successes in the rink and on the football field, I was once again struggling in the classroom. It was a time at Hamilton where people were meant to suck it up. No one at Hamilton nor I talked about dyslexia, and I still didn't even have a focused idea about what it was. The teachers weren't dealing with it, and my parents were not dealing with it, so there was no way I could deal with it. When I was told about dyslexia in my junior year at Taft, I was also told that if I slept a certain way with my hands extended out to the sides of the bed, maybe that would help it. It does not help, I can assure you. But that was the level of information with which I was dealing.

It became clear that I had a learning disability, and, in hindsight, Hamilton was probably one of the worst schools in the world that I could have gone to with dyslexia because they had no interest in helping me. Working harder was not the issue. The issue was that I didn't know what I was being asked to do.

Barry Seaman did not know that I was dyslexic at the time, but he did remember borrowing textbooks from me and that's how he learned about my difficulties. "I, being the irresponsible one, would lose textbooks, and I would end up borrowing Charlie's for some class," Barry recalled. "I just noticed the things that he highlighted on the pages were not the high points of the argument. It should not have been the stuff that was stressed. I didn't say anything about it, but it was my first suspicion that there was something wrong with his learning process."

Even so, I never gave up hope. Sometimes, though, my hope was a little twisted—and yet prophetic. When I took the government course in my sophomore year at Hamilton, I wrote in my notebook, "Charles Wardell, the White House, Washington D.C." Why did I write it? I guess I wanted to get as far away from where I was as I could imagine. Never in a million years did I truly imagine that I would wind up in the White House.

I did learn how to drink at Hamilton. It was still a time when fraternities had outrageous parties. The Dekes led the festive way with such enthusiasm that eventually fraternities were banned at Hamilton. Next to the Deke house was a cemetery, and we used to have keg parties in the cemetery. One Sunday morning, I woke up in the cemetery to watch a funeral coming into it. The mourners never saw me, but they saw the paper cups, the kegs, and the party mess.

My teammates tried to help me academically. I was once offered the opportunity to cheat on a fine arts test. I could sit behind the guy and look over his shoulder. But I couldn't do it. That approach didn't sit well with me. I was going to make it on my own. Or not. I remember when I went to see my geology professor for extra help, and he just looked at me and said, "I don't know what you're trying to do here." That made two of us. He just threw his hands up in the air, and so I left as foggy about the subject as when I came in.

After my freshman year, I went home to spend the summer on Long Island. I told my father that I thought things weren't going so well at college and that, maybe, I should take a year off. My father simply said, "No, you're going back to Hamilton next year."

So, I went back. I had been dating a young woman I had known from high school who was at Smith, which is in Massachusetts. It's about two hundred miles to the east, and a three-and-a-half-hour car ride if you were hitchhiking over to see her, which I did. She was very gifted academically, and I was pretty much obsessed with her, but we grew apart. I also dated a young woman from Cazenovia Junior College, which at the time was located in a motel and has since folded.

"Cazenovia, both the town and the lake are absolutely gorgeous," Barry Seaman recalled, "and there are some beautiful homes around the lake. I don't remember the campus because usually what we did was get a bunch of guys in a car and drive down there, and we would go immediately to some bar in Cazenovia. Somebody would go off to one of the dorms and knock on the door and get a bunch of girls to come out. That's how it kind of worked. And the party began."

My Cazenovia girlfriend was the Cazenovia beauty queen when I was in my sophomore year, which was clearly the highlight of my Hamilton social life. That and being elected as co-captain of the hockey team at the end of my sophomore year. I was surprised because my leadership style on the ice was mostly about survival. I played hockey as hard as I could. It was the only thing at Hamilton that seemed to work for me—even with the losing scores. As I mentioned, the coaching staff did not lead the team well, and the administration really didn't care if we won or lost. We played in a third-grade building with a poor man's Zamboni, which was a tractor hooked up with two tanks on the underside that spat out water into the ice, which was then smoothed by the towels dragging behind the tractor.

I was surprised to be elected co-captain, which is a big honor on any team. The players did that. In the end, I never had a chance to serve in the role, though, because the college asked me to leave after my sophomore year was done. I knew that whatever I was trying to do wasn't working and, eventually, they called time on this play. So, to me, Hamilton was a depressing two years. And it took me a long time to get over it. Ironically, when I was working at the White House, I got a very warm letter from Hamilton asking me if I wanted to become part of the Hamilton alumni group in Washington D.C. I declined.

At the time I was disposed of by Hamilton, in June 1965, I was in real pain, intellectually and emotionally. I was adrift, and I didn't think this life thing would all work out. I had no idea that I would have a successful life ahead. I was thinking two things: the first was that I would never graduate from college. And the second was: what the hell was I going to do next?

Ironically, of the ten guys who were in my fraternity pledge group, six of us "left" Hamilton and wound up in Vietnam. In hindsight, I was amazed that Hamilton was so cavalier about expelling people and exposing us to the Vietnam draft which was not a death sentence at that point but close to it, giving a soldier a 1 in 10 chance of being killed or wounded, and a 100% chance he'd have PTSD if he survived the war—a condition which was only officially recognized in 1980. Your student draft exemption was also immediately disallowed if you "left" college.

Vietnam is where I would soon be heading myself. Indeed, this new path was a forced second beginning of my story. Surprisingly, I would discover fine qualities in an institution and in myself in a place where I had never expected to find them: the United States Army.

Chapter 3
"Everyone has his turn in the barrel."

I was twenty years old when I returned to Long Island for the summer of 1965 after being bounced from Hamilton. The following year I spent thinking about what I would do next. I really wanted to go back to college in the fall of 1966, and I was hoping that Hamilton would realize that they had made a terrible mistake and invite me to come back. When I interviewed at other colleges, I was told that until I could be re-accepted in the college that I had left, I could not apply to a new college. You had to be eligible for admission to the school that you left in order to transfer into another school. It was the college Catch-22.

I was depressed and more than a little desperate. I knew we were fighting a war in Vietnam. Since 1965, active American combat units had been dispatched to Vietnam and with that reality came another: a military draft. If I weren't in college, I could be in a war.

So, I kept busy. I worked in construction, and I was the football coach of the six-man team at the East Woods Country Day school, which I had once attended and where my younger brothers Chris and David were students. That job paid me $75 a month, which is worth about $751 today—so not a lot even then.

I lived at home, which was quite advantageous for me as well as for my family. My father was going through a tough time financially, so paying for me to go back to Hamilton would have been a stretch for him. My mother had gone back to work at Time, Inc., and so I would pick up my youngest brother David from school and help around the house until she came home.

For fun, I would scrimmage with the Long Island Ducks, a minor league hockey team in the Eastern Hockey League owned by Al and Renee Baron, from 1959 until 1973 when the Eastern League folded. I don't think I was ever officially on their roster. The team arena in Commack was small and had poor indoor heating, so the fans were often freezing cold in the stands. During one cold game, fans lit a bonfire in the arena. The owner of the team, Al Baron, joked, "Tonight's game is brought to you by the Smithtown Fire Department."

Chicken wire originally separated the players from the fans above the dasher boards. One night, a player jumped over the boards and punched a fan, which then prompted our owner to make another joke. "This is the only rink in organized hockey where the players stand on the ice and watch the fights in the stands," he said. Suffice to say, it was a long way from the NHL. I also worked as a driver. I had one regular customer who I would drive to Manhattan for her doctor's appointments. Other people would call me and say, "Hey, can you drive me to New York tomorrow? Or pick me up at the airport?" I wasn't ostracized by the community, but their perception of me was one of pity. "It's too bad. He's a great guy, but something's wrong with him."

I had a great time driving Jean Louis, a French guy, around the United States. Brad Miller, my friend Dwight's dad, hired me to drive him and Jean Louis to California—then down to Tijuana and back. We were gone for two and half months. A few cold beers and some long and happy nights were had along the way.

And cold beers were had when I got back to Long Island. To escape the uncertainty and the failure, I would go to the Sportsman's Bar in Huntington, which is about a five-minute drive north from Cold Spring Harbor where we lived. The musical genius Billy Joel used to play there as he was another Long Island guy. In fact, he called his first album Cold Spring Harbor, and I got to know him when I hung out there.

As winter slowly evolved into the spring of 1966, the Thomas family, who lived next door to us, asked me to perform an unusual service, given my academic background. They asked me if I would come over and read *The New York Times* newspaper aloud to the patriarch, Norman Thomas. Mr. Thomas was a fascinating man, then eighty years old, and very sharp of mind, but his eyesight was failing. He was a Presbyterian minister, socialist, and pacifist who had run six consecutive times for the U.S. presidency, beginning in 1928 as a candidate for the Socialist Party of America. His motto was, "I am not the champion of lost causes but the champion of causes not yet won." I could sympathize.

I was good friends with his grandson Evan, who would become a well-known journalist, historian, lawyer and the author of eleven books, so I agreed. I went over to Thomas's house and started reading *The New York Times* aloud, and I can tell you that reading aloud was never one of my great skills. And I was reading aloud to the august Norman Thomas, author of many learned books and himself a Princeton graduate. I would hang around after I had read enough, and Norman and I talked about why I had been asked to leave Hamilton. I told him that I didn't have a high enough average in any one course to be able to pick a major. And, frankly, the college thought that I never would.

Norman Thomas was most offended by their reasoning and said that it was a bunch of nonsense—with which I happened to agree. He then wrote a letter on my behalf to Lake Forest College in Illinois, a small, private liberal arts college on the shore of Lake Michigan, which had been founded by Presbyterian ministers in 1857.

As a Presbyterian minister himself with a high public profile, Thomas's letter got noticed, and I was admitted to Lake Forest as a student beginning in the September of 1966 because of Norman Thomas. They overlooked the fact that I had not been made eligible to go back to Hamilton. I was relieved and thrilled to have beaten the College Catch-22.

This is what goodness looked like.

This was a man from outside of my own family who took responsibility to help me, and he did so out of friendship and honor. He said he was going to do something for me, and he did it, and now I had a college to attend.

But life had other plans. I finally got a draft notice that spring, and so I appealed it with my father. We went to the South Shore of Long Island to a draft board that was composed of three guys, a fireman, a policeman, and a construction worker, and we made my case. I was going back to college. In August 1966, I received a letter from the U.S. government telling me my appeal had not been accepted, and that I had been drafted into the Army. They don't tell you why, but I knew why: that draft board where I made my appeal saw me as some privileged rich kid from the North Shore. I was most definitely not that, but it didn't matter. They were not going to let me escape. So, I was told to report to the Fort Hamilton, Brooklyn induction center on October 22, 1966. Lake Forest would have to wait.

That would also assume that I would get out of the Army alive because I was drafted to fight in the war the U.S. was waging in Vietnam. The Cold War that saw the democracy of the West in opposition to the Communism of the East drove U.S. actions and became the global policy of containment toward the Soviet Union. Containment was accompanied by the domino theory— meaning that, if dominoes are lined up in a row, and you knock over the first one, they will all fall down. So the thinking went with the dominoes of Communism. If we didn't contain one Communist country in a region, then they would all go over to the dark side. The U.S. had been advising the South Vietnamese since the late 1950s in their war against the Communist North. Each year, the U.S. was committing successively more resources to the war, and, by March 1965, President Lyndon B. Johnson had begun a three-year bombing campaign aimed at targets in North Vietnam. In that same month, U.S. Marines landed in South Vietnam as the first American combat troops to enter the country.

About a year before I had received my draft notice, President Lyndon B. Johnson called for another 500,000 American ground troops to be sent to Vietnam, which in turn increased the draft to 35,000 men each month.

My father, who was a patriotic man and a veteran of World War II and who had spent two years in the Pacific with the Navy with a PT boat squadron, said to me, "Look, you can do anything that's legal to avoid fighting in Vietnam. But if you do something illegal, such as go to Canada, then I would be enormously disappointed if you chose that path. If you want to be a conscientious objector and go to jail, go to jail. You can do anything the country allows you to do."

Did I think of heading to safety—and maybe to spend the rest of my life, at that—in hockey-loving Canada? No, I did not. I came from the World War II generation, and my country had asked me to serve. In my mind, there was only one answer to that request, and it was "Yes." It was my turn in the barrel.

The expression comes, appropriately, from a military joke involving a barrel with a hole in it, which was used for a sexual act. A new recruit is shown this barrel and told he can use it every day but for Tuesday. "Why not Tuesdays?" he asks, and they tell him: "Because it's your turn in the barrel." The phrase evolved to mean that everyone must take their turn at an unpleasant or undesirable task, and that was what I was about to do.

So, on October 22, 1966, my mother and I set out from Cold Spring Harbor to the U.S. Army Induction Center at Fort Hamilton, Brooklyn. The journey was only about fifty miles, but traveling with my mother was an adventure. My mother was also dyslexic, and that's where I got it from. My mother lived in the same house for thirty years, and she couldn't pick out where the mailbox was. Her sense of direction left much to be desired, so I was out on the street, stopping people and asking them, "Do you know where Fort Hamilton is located?" I was fifteen minutes late for this first meeting with the Army, which everyone noticed because I was the last guy to walk into a packed room, and I thought to myself, with my mother's sense of direction, we're lucky we found Brooklyn, much less Fort Hamilton—the second largest military processing station in the country—but at least I had shown up.

There must have been two hundred people in the room. No one yelled or screamed at us, so the scene was different from what you might see in the Marine Corps in movies. The senior sergeant's tone was stern and serious, letting us know that we were now in the U.S. Army, and a whole new set of rules would apply to the way we lived.

They gave us an IQ test and, as I have done in the past, I did well on this one, too; while I never learned the score that I achieved, eventually its results would lead me to become an officer. But, right now, I was a private, a grunt, like everyone else.

When we were sworn in, I actually misspelled the United States on the form I had to sign, but that wasn't the issue that saw me punished. It was my name.

"Wardell, Charles W. B. Three!" The senior sergeant scanned the room for this character with the fancy name. I suppose they were not used to seeing names like mine with numbers after them. So, I identified myself, and the sergeant yelled at me to get outside and cut the grass. That was my first act in the U.S. Army. The lawn at the Fort Hamilton Induction Center is the size of a football field. I was having to mow it because of my name, which I guess sounded like a rich kid's name to the sergeant who wanted to knock me down a peg or two, but I was no rich kid. I mean, I had been drafted into the U.S. Army! It was clear to me from that moment on that different rules were going to apply in this world. It would turn out that some of them would suit me very well.

Everyone inducted on that day was sent to Fort Dix in New Jersey—except for forty of us. All of the guys with me were Black, save for one other white guy, and we were sent to Fort Ord, California. So, we flew out to Fort Ord, which is on Monterey Bay, 115 miles south of San Francisco. We were processed into the U.S. Army at Fort Ord in this gorgeous spot overlooking the blue Pacific that was physically closer to Vietnam than it was to Fort Dix, New Jersey. As we were being processed, we were asked where we wanted to be stationed. And, for some reason that to this day I still don't understand, I volunteered to go to Vietnam. I said to myself, "Well, that's why I got drafted. I might as well go to Vietnam because I'm in the Army, and that's where the war is."

It was one of the biggest mistakes I have ever made, and I've made a lot of them. I didn't know it at the time, but I was about to go across the country on an Army adventure as I got trained to do what I had volunteered to do. That was to go to war. To go to Vietnam. And to do my damnedest to come back alive. In the autumn of 1966, my next port of call after Fort Ord, California was

Fort Lewis, Washington, about ten miles south of Tacoma. The Army had reopened barracks at Fort Lewis, which they had not used since the Korean War. Not only was our housing musty, but these barracks had coal fire furnaces, so we had to shovel coal to stay warm and dry in a place where temperatures drop below 50 F on 299 days of the year and the annual rainfall is 48.6 inches, the highest in the country. "Dank" is the word to describe the place.

Basic training lasts about three months, so I got to experience a Pacific Northwest winter, which was nothing like I had ever seen on Long Island and nothing like I was going to see in Vietnam. When spring 1967 finally landed, I was heading off to join the Army's Navy because I had volunteered for this when I went into the regular Army, with a three-year commitment, unlike the regular draftee, who only had a two-year commitment. So I signed up for an assignment to the Army's maritime fleet of vessels.

Interestingly enough, the Army has more floating craft than the actual U.S. Navy. I was sent to my third fort in six months, this next one being Fort Eustis in Newport News, Virginia to learn how to drive boats. I became the coxswain of an LCM, also known as a "landing craft mechanized," which is a large boat that is used to move heavy equipment. I also learned how to work tugboats as well.

I had grown up around boats, sailing as a kid on Long Island Sound, and my Army instructors were great. They were all military people and their leadership was something that I've always had huge respect for. This was the "can do" part of the military. My instructors were hardworking people who were good at their crafts and knew how to teach them. They could not have been more pleasant—in a military way—which means they kept to the task at hand, but they made sure you understood what was being asked of you and helped you to do it. The Army could have taught the people at Hamilton College a thing or two about teaching. I liked being on the water where the ocean did the work for you instead of your legs. I also liked the class and, out of the one hundred students in that class, I actually came out on top. Up until this point in my life, outside of hockey, everything had been tainted by the slow drip of failure. Now, in a place I had not expected to find it, I had great instructors, and I responded to them in a way that made them come to see me as the best student in the class.

Of course, I had no idea that this honor was coming. The company mustered. They said to us, "Private First Class Wardell, please step forward." I did so, wondering what I had done to get singled out. Then the lieutenant who was head of the transportation training company announced that I was the top graduate in the class. My Army instructors had nominated me for the award, and this was the first tangible sign in my life, off the ice, that maybe I had something in me that everyone else had missed.

Well, not quite true. It was the first time since I graduated from East Woods school at the end of eighth grade when I received a "special award." At East Woods, I didn't qualify for the standard graduation awards that they handed out to the worthy. I guess that they didn't want me to feel left out, so I got a letter from the faculty saying that I was a good guy. And while I had been elected co-captain of the Hamilton hockey team, that was a bittersweet achievement because I never got to serve in that role. I was expelled. So, this marked the first time I was being honored straight up for something I had achieved better than anybody else.

I was, as you can imagine, elated. The Army gave me a porcelain beer mug that proclaimed me as the top graduate in the class, and my father put it on a shelf in our home in Cold Spring Harbor. Achieving this honor was a kind of redemption for me. It was the beginning of my being judged against a broad group of people who were my peers and proving that I could succeed. Winning this honor was a very big deal, and having something at last on my father's shelf was a point of pride, even if it was a beer mug—which I have found to be an especially useful vessel at times.

As part of my achievement, the Army awarded me a three-day pass. I could fly home to Long Island and celebrate with my family. When I got to the small airport near Fort Eustis, Virginia, they had one seat left on the airplane. There was an Army major who wanted that seat, though, and there was me, an enlisted grunt. So, they gave the seat to the major, and my three-day pass became a Saturday-afternoon-until-Sunday pass. I never forgot that, either. Was this major a better man than me? Who knows? He held a higher rank and, to the Army, that was the deciding factor. So, I had seen leadership at its best among my instructors and bureaucracy at its most predictable at the airport.

Come Up Big

My day-plus visit home was short, but it was probably the best in my life, so far, with my parents and siblings busting proud of me if not a little bit shocked at my success. I graduated from Fort Eustis with top honors, and the IQ test that I had taken when inducted into the Army had impressed them. This combination spurred me to apply to go to the officers' candidate school (OCS).

It was not about ambition, it was about survival. I knew that if I didn't do something to keep myself in Army schools, then I would soon be driving an LCM on the Mekong Delta in Vietnam. I figured that attending the OCS would postpone that riverine adventure. If I had any strategy at all at that time, it was that if I kept going to Army schools, then maybe the war would end before I finished my Army schooling. I, who had previously seen school as a form of personal torture, eagerly applied to the OCS, and I got accepted into the Armor School in Fort Knox, Kentucky.

When I arrived at the Armor School, OCS candidates were leaning out of barracks windows screaming at us new guys, "You'll be sorry!"

This was my fourth fort in less than a year, and I was not sorry at all. I was impressed by this school as well, since this was the first time in my life I had strung together two academic successes in a row. Maybe, just maybe, things were looking up for me even if I was looking at going to war. As I made my way to the Armor School, I thought about how different the Army was from college. They were paying keen attention to me and saw what I could do. And then, they encouraged me to do more.

It was the summer of 1967, the summer of love, and while you couldn't call it love, exactly, I was very happy with my relationship with the United States Army Armor School. It had been established on October 1, 1940, in Fort Knox and was so big at 172 square miles that it covered three counties in Kentucky.

My time of learning at the Armor School was a tough six months, and only about half the candidates graduated from the course. It was no joke, and, in wartime, it was particularly no joke. The cadre that ran the Armor class were serious men who had come from what was beginning to look like a very tough war in Vietnam. On our first day, the first sergeant of the training class said, "Youse men will either graduate or quituate."

We all took that very seriously, and some of my colleagues did "quituate." We didn't have the tradition of the Navy SEALS where you ring the bell to say you've had enough. At the Armor School, you could go in to see the commanding officer at any time and say that you were done. And you were done, but not with the Army, for then you would be most likely on your way to Vietnam.

Every two months, we had this vetting period where you either were told to stay, or you were given orders to leave. It was a big sweat as I had already been asked to leave one academic institution. Would I be asked to leave this one? And sent to the jungles of Vietnam?

The OCS was academic and run by officers. The

Armor School teaches you the A-Zs of armored combat. We did everything from hard physical training to all the different types of marksmanship: from field firing, where you fire at targets at various ranges to record firing, where instructors watch and record your shots.

We used the M16 rifle, which was lighter than the previous version, known as the M14, and which was made of wood. The M16 was made of plastic and weighed about nine pounds. It carried a much smaller round and once the bullet hit a target it tumbled end over end. Other guns sent rounds that spun and went through you, but this one tumbled into you. It had a huge impact. Some people died from shock when they got hit with a round.

The M16 had a selector switch that would let you choose a single shot, a three-round burst, or a fully automatic option. In the later versions, they removed the fully automatic option because, when fully automatic, the rifle climbs to the right, and you don't hit much. And it gets incredibly hot.

The M-16 rifle can hold a thirty-round load and a sling. Its maximum range is 3,600 meters, which is about two-and-a-quarter miles, but it was most effective at under 550 meters—about the length of six football fields. It was an immensely powerful beast, and I was a pretty good shot.

We had bayonet training, and hand-to-hand combat training and, as the armor in the school's name indicates, we learned a lot about armored vehicles and artillery.

We had to take written tests based upon the tactical

operation of armor: how to drive armored vehicles and tanks and how to use those guns and artillery. I was just fine with the tests because they were practical exams about tactics. Questions were like "How would you use armor to support infantry in this situation?" It wasn't presented by a very smart and snobby professor who was loftily giving us the nuance of French philosophic thought in the eighteenth century; it was delivered by officers who had been in combat in Vietnam. They wanted us to succeed because, if we didn't, we'd be dead.

They would say things like, "Troops, you're gonna need this. It's a 105-millimeter artillery piece. And this is how it works." We also had the 155-millimeter mechanized piece.

We would watch to learn how they all worked. So, from a practical point of view, I did not find it difficult to follow, and I graduated from OCS as a second lieutenant. I had learned basic leadership skills and tactical planning. In pretty short order, I had gone from being an expelled college student to a highly trained warrior.

Some of my OCS classmates were assigned to Germany, and many of them never went to Vietnam. I went to Vietnam because I had volunteered to go there—but not quite yet. Now, in December 1967, I was on my way to Fort Leonard Wood in Missouri where I would spend the next seven months. I was assigned to a basic training battalion where we trained incoming troops. The student had now become an instructor in the United States Army.

It was in this new role, as a teacher myself—something I could never have imagined—that I learned about my own abilities as a leader. I learned about the qualities of leadership that best suited me and, as it would turn out, best suited the troops. I began to realize that, if I had thirty soldiers in front of me, I could articulate what our mission was, and I could get them to understand that we had to do it all together. It was everything that had not been given to me until I reached the Army. I wanted to make sure that we were all in this together, having spent most of my life learning on my own with no help to understand the subject at hand. I wanted everyone to understand that no one was on his own. When I was in Vietnam in one particularly difficult operation we worked with the 11th Armored Cavalry Regiment. And a young American soldier came up to me smiling and said, "You're Lieutenant Wardell. And I gotta tell you, you are the best leader I've ever had." I trained him when I was at Fort Leonard Wood.

Why would he say this to me? Well, when I was at Fort Leonard Wood, I began to realize that, if I were going to get anywhere in life, I would have to find an offbeat way to exude confidence because the traditional methods I had been shown did not do that. I had been exposed to humor at home. My mother had a great sense of humor and shared golden nuggets of wisdom that had me howling and still do, but she also reminded me that there were limits to humor: "There's a line beyond which the Wardells don't go." So, I began to develop my own sense of humor and learned to teach through humor, which reduces anxiety. This was critical among troops facing war, and it boosts participation, and it increases the students' confidence in the material that is being presented. If you can laugh, you can learn.

I also took care that, when I asked others to do something, I let them know that I was also doing what I asked them to do. It was important to me to treat others fairly, having not been dealt with fairly in my life by people teaching me.

A good example of that happened at Fort Leonard Wood. We had failed a rifle inspection. All our training rifles were dirty. When the battalion's first sergeant came through our company headquarters, I was sitting on the floor with the enlisted men cleaning rifles. The sergeant looked at me and he said, "I've never seen that before."

I was an officer, helping to clean rifles, so we could pass the next inspection. I also did that in Vietnam. I took my turn. Sometimes, it was things that officers did not normally do. For example, I took my turn walking point in Vietnam. The point man's role is to be the eyes and ears of the patrol as you move forward and to watch for enemy soldiers. It is often considered the most dangerous position in a patrol because you're the first guy who's going to get enemy fire. Officers don't walk point, but I did.

At night, I also went out on LPs—listening and observation posts. This is not something that company leaders were required to do, but I also learned to give my men an out. I said to my team, "Everybody has one opportunity to say no. No questions asked." Everybody had the same single chance to say no. Troops hated to be commanded to do something that they didn't want to do. Having a choice, having an out, was greatly appreciated. The first sergeant in the training battalion that I was assigned to was Sergeant Wells who had been an advisor in Vietnam. He said he respected me more than the other second lieutenants, and I was rated well. I was slated to go to the First Infantry Division in Vietnam, known as "The Bloody Red One" because of their light green badge featuring a red number 1 on a light green field. And, as the Army's oldest continuously serving division, they were the first to land in France in World War I and they landed on Omaha Beach on D-Day in 1944. Sergeant Wells said, "Lieutenant, you do not want to go to a leg (i.e., on foot and not motorized) Infantry Division in Vietnam. You're probably not going to survive. Why don't you think about going to on to the Special Warfare School at Fort Bragg, North Carolina?"

I had not thought about making an application to the Special Warfare School but, if I could stick to my stay-in-school strategy and if it could keep me in the U.S. a little longer, I was all for it. As a personal favor to me, Sergeant Wells called the armor branch in the Pentagon. In Wells' first tour of Vietnam, he served with an officer who was now the head of company grade assignments for the armor branch. Sergeant Wells was the reason I was accepted to the Special Warfare School.

So, my friends went to calvary units or to infantry units in Vietnam from Fort Leonard Wood, and they did not all come back. And I went to the John F. Kennedy Special Warfare School at Fort Bragg, North Carolina in June 1968, my sixth port of call in less than two years. I was going to learn how to be an advisor with "host country" troops, something I had never imagined I would be when I was cutting the grass at Fort Hamilton's induction center.

The instructions were tailored to the landscape of the battle that was forthcoming. It got your attention. Many of our instructors were Vietnamese nationals and combat veterans, and they would say, "You will see this in Vietnam and, if you don't react quickly enough, it will kill you." We knew that they were telling the truth because they had seen it.

The teachers at the Special Warfare School were not just about giving us physical training. One thing that I still find to be amusing is how people equate rugged physical training with toughness. I believe that toughness is mental, so I never estimate anyone by their brawn.

The Special Warfare School had been created to teach advisors how to fight with host country troops. At the same time, it was also a touch more relaxed. For example, instead of sleeping in a barracks, I lived in Moon Hall, a classier joint known as an "army hotel" that was named for Captain Walter Hugh "Wally" Moon who was killed in 1961 while a POW in Laos. On April 22, 1961, Captain Moon's battalion was hit by a heavy artillery barrage and then rapidly flanked by the enemy. The battalion commander announced that the Americans had been cut off; then the perimeter collapsed, and the Pathet Lao guerrillas overran the battalion positions and captured Captain Moon.

He tried to escape twice during his imprisonment,

and, on his second attempt, he was wounded in the chest and head. His head injury and his imprisonment had caused him to become mentally distressed and, after several months of persecution, he was executed in his prison quarters on July 22, 1961.

So, living in a place named after a soldier who had endured what Captain Moon had endured, we all knew what was in front of us. The agony wasn't so much the day-to-day agony of waiting; it was the agony of what we were going to face. We had received a lot of instruction in the tactics of the North Vietnamese. The Viet Cong treated the peasants in the villages with respect, who in turn gave them food, shelter, and hiding places. They also instilled fear in the peasants that the Americans and South Vietnamese would take their land away.

They also picked battles that they had a chance of winning. Their weapons included daggers, swords, and explosives captured from the Americans. They made booby traps from pointed bamboo sticks that would impale you when triggered. They wore no uniform and could not be found in any particular location, and they used tunnels to escape into the jungle. Their combat cells were very small so that, if we captured any of them, they could not give much information about the bigger plan.

The North Vietnamese regulars wore uniforms. Both they and the Viet Cong were incredibly brutal to villages that supported the South. They beheaded people. They would take pregnant women, hang them upside down, and cut them open. It was terrible.

Even with all that dark and dismal intel, I wasn't

prepared for living in the jungle. Life in the green hills of North Carolina, with the summer thermometer traveling between 80 and 100 F and just a few tornadoes to bother you, is not at all like life in the monsoon season in the jungles of Southeast Asia.

I was also taught to speak Vietnamese, which was tough because, as you might imagine, I sometimes find English a challenge. In fact, when it comes to speaking foreign languages, my basic strategy is to speak English louder and slower. I tried to speak some Vietnamese although, whenever I found myself in a tough situation in Vietnam, and my Vietnamese counterparts would tell me to speak English. Even so, I graduated in the top ten percent of my class. This was another affirmation of my ability, but it came with a great burden because now I really was going to Vietnam as an officer.

And so I was assigned to the 5th ARVN Division as an advisor. The year 1968 had been pretty awful for the United States in Vietnam. Come the end of January, when the Vietnamese celebrated the lunar holiday Tet, the Viet Cong took advantage of this festive time to launch a massive attack on the South. The Viet Cong assaulted more than one hundred towns and cities across South Vietnam, but the South Vietnamese and the American troops succeeded in repelling them. By the end of the Tet Offensive, more than 37,000 Viet Cong troops had been killed, including some of their top guys. More than half a million civilians had been displaced, and more than 2,500 Americans had been killed. The U.S. public turned increasingly against the war, which is part of the reason that President Lyndon B. Johnson turned down the U.S. Commander General William Westmoreland's request to build on the "success" of Tet by having him send in an additional 200,000 troops, which would have put our troop numbers in Vietnam at nearly three-quarters of a million.

It would not work politically, given the mood in the U.S. In fact, at the beginning of the year, before the Tet Offensive, twenty-eight percent of Americans were opposed to the war in Vietnam. After Tet, that number rose to forty-two percent. It didn't look as if the war could be won anytime soon, which Johnson had envisaged doing earlier in the year. In fact, now he saw the writing clearly on the wall and, in March 1968, he announced that he would not seek a second term as president.

The number of Americans opposed to the war would rise even higher after the My Lai Massacre in that same month. Soldiers from the American Division killed two hundred civilians in the Vietnamese village called My Lai, which did much damage to the Army both in Vietnam and at home. Americans were shocked to learn that our own soldiers would kill civilians so wantonly or, more accurately, that they were obeying orders to do so given by higher ups.

In the U.S., things went from very bad to awful. On April 4, 1968, Martin Luther King Jr. was assassinated in Memphis, Tennessee. The man whose "I have a dream speech" had fueled the hopes and dreams of millions had been shot dead while standing on the balcony of his motel room by an escaped fugitive. King's killing set off a wave of rioting across the country with the violence of those riots affecting more than one hundred cities and killing more than forty Americans.

Just two months after King had been assassinated, Robert Kennedy spoke to a crowd who were supporting his sweep in the California primary in his run to win the Democratic Party nomination for president and to take up the work of his own assassinated brother, John F. Kennedy, had left unfinished. But he, too, was shot and killed by an assassin. The United States was in deep mourning for these men—and for itself.

Things kept getting worse. When the Democrats held their convention in Chicago in August 1968, people opposed to the war in Vietnam surged into the city. The mayor of Chicago told the police to be tough with the war protesters who shouted "the world is watching" while the Chicago PD bashed them with nightsticks and convulsed them with tear gas.

So it was in this context that twenty-two-year-old me was about to head off to fight a war that had changed on many fronts. I was certainly aware of this, but I had also spent most of the last two years in the Army learning how to do what I had sworn to do, and which they thought that I could do—and do well. I believe in "comrades in arms," and I couldn't let them down now. Now the test was going to happen. But I was not traveling there with comrades in arms. I was on my own.

In truth, I had no idea what I was about to step into in Vietnam. But this is where I went, what I saw, what I learned, and what I did. This is what happened.

Chapter 4
"Sleeping sentries get you killed."

After I graduated from the John F. Kennedy Special Warfare School, I was given a thirty-day leave before I was assigned to Vietnam. I went home and one thing I recall is telling my father that I did not want to be buried in my uniform should I not survive Vietnam. He said, "Okay." That was it.

I hung out and spent time with my brothers, but I always had my destination in mind. I was going off to war because I had flunked out of college. I hadn't had any great wins except that I suddenly found myself an officer, going to what was called a hot war. I wasn't going as a supply clerk. I was going to confront the enemy. I had no instinctive sense of what was ahead because I had never done it before. And, if I had known the truth of it all, I would have gone anyway. I did not travel to Vietnam with an American Army unit because I was a replacement. So, I was on my own. I said an emotional goodbye to my mother and my sister Wendy at John F. Kennedy Airport in New York, feeling that I would see them again one day but not knowing in what state I would be. Somehow, I knew I would not die in Vietnam.

I soon realized that in my distraction, I had forgotten to bring any Army socks, so I went out and bought socks and put them in the little brown suitcase I was traveling with. I then flew on a commercial airliner to San Francisco.

I landed in San Francisco and spent the night there before reporting to the Oakland Army Terminal. I was bused to a chartered Pan Am flight and flown to Vietnam. I sat in the center seat on a Boeing 707 and flew for seventeen hours to Southeast Asia, surrounded by strangers, all of us going to Vietnam, with a brief stopover at Clark Air Force Base in the Philippines. There were even flight attendants on board, which made the experience even more surreal. The U.S. Air Force gave these flight attendants the rank of second lieutenants, the same rank as me, which meant that if they were captured (a risk for sure), they could claim protection as prisoners of war under the rules of the Geneva Convention. But they were not wearing Army uniforms. They still wore those white gloves and baby blue "overseas caps."

    We landed at Tan Son Nhut Air Base in Saigon and, when the doors of the plane finally opened, my body was overcome with this blast of heat and the stench and stickiness of being cooped up in that metal tube with all these other humans for many hours. The heat and the smell of Vietnam just knocks you off your feet. I was finally "in country."

    Saigon was a great French flavored city in Vietnam, seasoned with lovely French architecture and food. There was a French golf course there, built by the Michelin rubber people but if you hit your ball off the green, you couldn't look for it outside the barbed wire that surrounded the course because of the lurking booby traps—very different from your standard sand traps.

    My first stop in country was MACV, which is the Military Assistance Command Vietnam, where I was processed and had a one-day orientation. I was assigned to my advisory team, and I was essentially told to get out there and support the South Vietnamese. I was issued a green U.S. Army uniform and combat boots to go with my non-Army socks. They were all new, and so I and all the others who had arrived with me were known as FNGs. Fucking New Guys.

We were then dispatched all over the country. I was assigned to the 5th Division of the Army of the Republic of Vietnam (ARVN), Third Regiment, Second Battalion. I had never been in combat but, suddenly, I was an adviser to Vietnamese soldiers who had been fighting for years.

I flew in a helicopter for the first time in Vietnam, which was nerve-wracking given the rattle and the noise. We landed at a midpoint where I was told I was going to be moved to my unit in the field the next day. I still had my little brown suitcase with me, and I slept on the floor of an old Vietnamese building with no mattress and no pillow and then got up the next morning in my uniform to board another helicopter. I flew down to Lam Son, which is a thousand miles south of Hanoi, and joined the 5th ARVN Division.

I was part of an advisory team led by Captain Deere and Sergeant Hitchman. I went in to see the captain, and he explained what they were doing in Vietnam. After all the talk and all the training, it now became very real. I was going to be here doing what I had trained to do for the next year. Or maybe for less.

Captain Deere was on his second tour. He had been a ROTC officer, and he and his wife just had a child at home whom he had never met. He was the officer who yelled at me when we were moving out to "Get that weapon off your shoulder!" I had my rifle slung over my shoulder, and Deere made me have it ready with a round in the chamber so I would be ready when the enemy popped up from anywhere. I used that line on my soldiers myself.

I moved to the field to join my unit. On my first night in the field, we were mortared and probed by the North Vietnamese or the Viet Cong; it was hard to tell. We were "in contact." We were dug into foxholes, and I remember Major Dinh, who was my Vietnamese counterpart, telling me to put my back against the dirt of our hole. It would give me a better chance of living. Major Dinh was a young rising star in the 5th ARVN division. He spoke French and good enough English. He had a wife and two kids who traveled with us. He also, I would discover, had multiple girlfriends.

I was ordered to call in for a Medevac—medical evacuation—helicopter. It would take the wounded South Vietnamese troops to the hospital. I was so nervous calling coordinates that I could barely turn the pages on the codebook that encoded the coordinates of our location. So, when the chopper finally came, I ran out into the LZ, or the landing zone, to guide the chopper in and then help to load the wounded onboard. There were about thirty killed, as well, but no Americans died. Then I ran back into the hole and tried to stay alive. That was my first day in combat.

I had a weapon, but I didn't fight. I didn't know what to do. I stood up at one point, and Sergeant Hitchman grabbed the back of my pack. He yelled, "Get down! Jesus Christ!" I got down. It took me a couple of firefights to actually shoot back at the people shooting at me.

It was all terrifying. I thought that, if every day would be like this, there was no chance that I would survive. I was in shock. It took everything I had within me to stop myself from crying. One of the worst things was loneliness. I didn't go over to Vietnam with dozens of buddies in the 82nd Airborne. I didn't even go over with anyone from the Special Warfare School. I went over by myself before joining a group of people I'd never met before as the FNG. I did notice that the morning after my first harrowing day in the field, my new green uniform had faded quite a bit. I didn't look like an FNG anymore. But I was still very much one.

Being by myself, with the Vietnamese people whose language I really didn't speak and who were much better trained and had been fighting here for years, might sound as if I felt doomed. Ironically, I was used to being alone and to not knowing what I was doing. I was used to being the only kid in French class who didn't know French. And now, here I was once again, not knowing what to do next. That was a saving grace.

We had the same communications system as they did in World War II. We would fire up a ham radio and talk to ham radio operators around the world who volunteered to hook us up to the U.S. phone system.

The one time I tried to do that, after having been in Vietnam about six months, was an exercise in comedy. I lived in Cold Spring Harbor, New York, but the ham operator thought it was Cold Spring, New York. I got word that my family had moved and had left no forwarding address. I knew it wasn't true but, if it had happened on day two of my deployment, I wouldn't have laughed like I did then at the mistake. I would have been beside myself with worry.

There were a lot of questions running through my young head in Vietnam. I thought, "Can I live through this? Can I handle this? Can I deal with this world? Could I be a coward?" When you're fighting a war with host country nationals whose language you don't speak, and who don't speak English very well, it's natural to feel very lonely as you sort out that stuff by yourself.

The Vietnamese called the American advisers *co van* and, as time passed and we got into tough situations, I could hear Vietnamese troops screaming *"Co van! Co van!"* which meant, "Shoot the advisor, don't shoot me." Our role as advisers was to connect with the tactical operations center and 5th ARVN division to bring in artillery and aircraft—essentially to bring in all the power we had to bear on the battle at hand.

Each day was different. I might get up in the morning and move out, or I might stay in one location all day. I might get orders to move out for thirty days into a new AO—which is "area of operations." And, so, we'd start moving out. Mostly we'd walk but, occasionally, we would get the word that "This mission will include motorized transport," and that meant we would move out on helicopters.

As time in the field passes, you really begin to deal with fear and with uncertainty along with the other issues that field duty presents. Relationships get strained, and our diet didn't help soothe the strain. We ate much differently than the other U.S. troops who got a hot meal every day. The food was Vietnamese, and it led to diarrhea. We did have medics to check up on us, but we didn't have the top-notch medical care that the regular troops had. We were living off the land along with the families of the Vietnamese soldiers who traveled with us much of the time.

During the days we were operating in the field, we stopped at around four o'clock in the afternoon, and we would dig in. We'd set up an NDP, a night defensive position. We'd string our razor wire that had sharp little blades on it along the perimeter of our position and put out our Claymore mines. The mines, developed in 1960, are about the size of a big cellphone and stand on small legs, but this little thing can blast seven hundred metal balls about three hundred feet and they are deadly. We'd also set out our LPs—listening posts—and the troops would go out on patrol to see if we could locate the enemy. I went out occasionally to see where the enemy was. Most of the time, they weren't there, but we didn't know that. It felt like they were everywhere. Waiting. Watching. Aiming for me.

If the North Vietnamese were really going to hit us hard, they would begin their attack at three in the morning by blowing whistles. They had little strips of phosphorus on the back of their helmets so that they could see one another in the dark, and they would come straight at us.

If you survived the night, then you would help to pack up everything and move out the next day. We would get dirty, and we would get bitten by bugs and develop rashes. Our three kit essentials were water, ammo, and toilet paper because we had constant intestinal issues from eating Army C-rations or Vietnamese food. The C-ration had 3,700 calories and was intended to feed you during operations of three to twenty-one days. The C-rations were pretty much the same as they had been in the Korean War. We'd have hard bread along with a main course such as canned spaghetti and meatballs, beef stew, or franks and beans. There would also be crackers, some chocolate, or hard candy, chewing gum and coffee, and a pack of cigarettes—yes, despite the fact the Surgeon General had warned of their hazards in 1964, but what could be worse than where we were?

I also carried the poems of Robert Frost in my backpack, and I would read them for emotional support. The one that resonated most with me was Frost's very short poem called "A Question":

> *A voice said, Look me in the stars*
> *And tell me truly, men of earth,*
> *If all the soul-and-body scars*
> *Were not too much to pay for birth.*

It was very uncomfortable, very lonely, and very difficult to do the right thing. I wrote a lot of letters home, and my family wrote to me. I was looking at one recently, and this is what I said to my parents then:

> *Dear Ma and Dad,*
> *I'm not nearly as tired as I was the last time I*

wrote. I didn't want to worry you, but I just can't keep all that to myself. I find I get extremely depressed, and I really don't know what to do. I really can't get along with any "Capt.," and the living conditions, weather, bugs, dirt, take some getting used to.

After Sat. my nerves are tough to control. On our next operation we went back to the same place. All the ARVN greats sat around and slept ETC, and I kept trying to put out security ETC, but no one seemed at all interested. We are going to build that compound, but I don't think it will be too bad. It is too easy to avoid and not important enough for Charlie to pay the price—hopefully.

So far, I haven't gotten any mail, but we can't pick it up as often as I'd like. I hope the address I'm giving is correct. I can't think of anything I might need, except a break at the Paris Peace Talks. I said I was looking forward to Vietnam, and now I'd love to come home for a cold beer.

My best to everyone and all the boys at Taft.

Love, Chuck.

My mention of Taft in that letter to my family was a code to them that I was OK. However, I didn't consider myself a good officer because I was as scared as the guy next to me who I was meant to be leading. Warfare is an extraordinarily complex matrix, and so is leading men in war. But, over time, I got the hang of it. And Sergeant Hitchman, who survived the war, was a tremendous help to me, using his experience and skill to keep me sane and safe. He was a very good man, and I learned a lot from him about how to stay cool and focused on keeping yourself and your team alive.

We would conduct small operations where twelve of us would go out on missions. It was terrifying, being out there in the jungle with every inch of space around you possibly lethal. I made myself do it, and I would feel guilty about not doing it well enough. That feeling never goes away. It's one telling you that maybe, just maybe, you could have done more.

And so, you begin to adjust. I began to feel what I see today as great sadness though it didn't strike me that way at the time. It felt more like great emptiness. I had spent seven months in the field, and I fought against the Viet Cong and, as we went north up into the Cambodia border region of Vietnam, we fought against the Third North Vietnamese Division.

They were also known as the Yellow Star Division in the People's Army of Vietnam (PAVN), first formed from the Viet Cong (VC) and PAVN units in September 1965. The first commanding officer and political officer of the division were veteran warriors, Colonel Giáp Văn Cương and Colonel Dang Hòa.

It wasn't all fighting, of course, and some of it was quite surreal. There was a soldier from New Jersey who brought his girlfriend over to Vietnam. She obtained her visa from Air France in Paris and flew from Paris on to Saigon. You could fly into Vietnam during the whole war as if it were a vacation destination. Air France had a regularly scheduled flight. The soldier's girlfriend was with this guy in a camp up near the Cambodian border.

She stayed there for four or five months. In all of the Vietnamese units, the families traveled with us. I remember once taking a sick child to one of our medics. The Vietnamese soldiers' girlfriends who traveled with us used to call me "star movie." Perfect for a guy with dyslexia. My boss, Captain Deere, was the head of our advisory team, the A-team, but he rotated out in the autumn of 1968. When they left, you did not know if you would ever see these people again. When he left our team, they didn't replace him for a long time. So, I was leading the team for most of my time in the field. I tried to be upbeat, and my upbeat attitude was well received. My troops believed in me, and I did the best I could. We did not take unnecessary risks.

In April 1969, Captain Deere's replacement finally came to us. He was a major who was a complete nut. He wasn't military in bearing or behavior; he was very self-serving, and he was arbitrary. He would say things to me such as, "Walk the perimeter tonight, Lieutenant. You're gonna go here, and then go there, and so on." It was insane.

I wasn't going to walk the perimeter and get myself killed. This guy had just arrived in the country and didn't have a clue about what we were up against. He was also terribly condescending to the South Vietnamese. This jerk of an officer had just been there less than two months as the commanding officer. Major Dinh, who was my Vietnamese counterpart whom I'd grown to respect and who had grown to respect me for how I had handled myself under fire, did not like him.

And so, one day, the Vietnamese shot him in the

legs. He went down screaming and he was yelling at me to call in a Medevac. But, trying not to be too helpful, we evacuated him not in a chopper, but fittingly, in a good old Jeep. This arrogant officer was the worst. He was a swaggering idiot whose incompetence would have gotten all of us killed had Major Dinh had not taken measures to stop him.

This "same team" shooting never got investigated. If a private threw a grenade into the hooch of his commanding officer and "fragged" him, then that would get investigated. But there was one round fired in our sector that day, and it hit the major. The major thought he had been hit by a sniper, and he got a Purple Heart for being wounded. Maybe he even thought of himself as a hero.

I found one of the more troubling aspects of Army leadership traits in Vietnam was that career officers had to get decorated. So, they had six months of rotations in and out of the field. If you were a career officer, you had to have a battalion command. So, every six months, we'd have a new company commander rotate in, so they could get their ticket punched, as in combat, and get their medal.

That was very hard on people like me because we weren't career officers. And I didn't give a damn if I got my ticket punched or not. That major who the Vietnamese shot in the leg was only there for four months.

I remember moving out one morning in this swampy land that was muddy, buggy, and generally shitty. The 5th ARVN started taking fire. When that happened, we would get on the AN/PRC-25, commonly called the "Prick 25" radio, and call the TOC—tactical operations center—to say, "We are in contact at this time."

The Prick 25 was developed in the late 1950s, and it was something of a miracle. The radio had solid-state circuitry, was water resistant, simple to operate, and easy to maintain. The handset, though, was not actually water resistant, so radio operators would use the battery pack's clear plastic wrapping to protect the handset from moisture and hold the wrapping in place with a rubber band. The batteries were good for two-to-three hours of heavy use or for several days if you didn't need to constantly use the radio.

The Prick 25 entered Vietnam in 1965. It was General Creighton Abrams, who was the head of Military Assistance Command Vietnam, who identified the Prick 25 as "the single most important tactical field item in Vietnam."

So, we called the tactical operations center and told them that we had made contact. The tech guys were anyone who merely supported soldiers in combat, such as staff people, mechanics, cooks, and such. But when a unit is in contact with the enemy, the rear echelon guys would get very excited because we had seen the enemy up close, and so, now, they could kill everybody. They started screaming at me: "What are you facing? What are you doing?" I didn't know. I said, "We're moving slowly because we got a lot of mud up to our knees, and even our chests, along with all the water."

Suddenly, the whop-whop of the blades of a

"Charlie" command and control helicopter from our headquarters was above us. An officer came up on my radio.

"You're all bunched up. Spread out!"

I said, "Roger that. We're doing the best we can in the swamp we're in."

He said, "Order your troops to spread out."

And I said, "Come down here, and do it yourself." His response was a "click." The call was over.

Now, if I had been a career officer, that would have ended my career, but I was a draftee. However, the story illustrates two types of leadership: one on the ground and, the other, literally up in the air. I could not do what that officer ordered because it was impossible. He did not see that situation from where he was sitting, but I certainly did. And so, I was not going to ask my troops to do something we were certain to fail at, me included.

Leadership in Vietnam was very difficult because the situation in Vietnam was truly hopeless. When I first got there, I slowly realized that we weren't going to win. I knew the body count measure for victory was a joke and that was how the U.S. Army assessed progress: by how many "gooks" we had killed. Living in the field in Vietnam was enormously difficult. America built rear echelon palaces for its troops, but I was living in the jungle going *mano a mano* against the fighting machine that was the North Vietnamese for a hopeless cause. Trying to do the best that I could. We believed that we were doing the Lord's work in Vietnam. We were drafted, we were asked to be there, and we were fighting for our country to help the host

Come Up Big

country's nationals from being overtaken by the Communists. We didn't lose the war in the field because we had effective artillery, and we had top-notch aircraft. However, we were fighting a determined enemy.

My South Vietnamese driver poisoned me with a bottle of water on a hot day, and I ended up violently ill in the hospital. He had worked with us for six months, and we thought he was a loyal South Vietnamese soldier in the 5th ARVN division, but he turned out to be a Viet Cong operative who decided to poison his passenger. Me. They never acknowledged that he'd poisoned me but I never saw him again and heard that he did not have a happy ending.

My mother was at Time, Inc. and made a huge effort to track down what had happened to me because she thought, when I was moved out of the field into hospital, that I had been wounded. When she finally got through, she was told that I had excessive chronic diarrhea, which has since become a family joke.

There was a colonel, who was a senior advisor to the ARVN, who had fought in World War II at the Battle of the Bulge with General Patton, and he was not joking at all when he took me aside in the officer's club one night and said, "Lieutenant. Don't try too hard."

At first, I was puzzled. Was he asking me to disobey orders? In a way, he was telling me to be discerning. He was really saying, "Don't do everything we tell you to do. Don't die over here."

I heard his message loud and clear, telling me to look out for myself. As I was still going to be in Vietnam for a few more months, I would take his advice to heart.

Now, the Battle of Hamburger Hill was no joke, nor am I making one, but I invoke it to reveal the kind of warfare we were up against in Vietnam. The battle happened in May 1969, and it was fought by the U.S. Army and ARVN forces against the People's Army of Vietnam. The Commies.

The heavily fortified Hill 937 was a ridge of the mountain Dong Ap Bia in central Vietnam about a mile from the border with Laos. It had little strategic value, but U.S. commanders ordered the 173rd Airborne Regiment up that hill to make a frontal assault to kill the enemy as that's how they measured progress. So, U.S. infantry troops moved up the steep hill against North Vietnamese troops who were dug in and who repeatedly pushed them back. The weather was bad, too.

U.S. Airborne troops eventually took the hill through direct assault and killed 630 enemy soldiers while 73 U.S. troops died and 370 were wounded. The hill got its name after U.S. Sergeant James Spears, a nineteen-year-old who fought in the battle and told reporters, "Have you ever been inside a hamburger machine? We just got cut to pieces by extremely accurate machine-gun fire." The U.S. Army abandoned the hill soon after it had been taken. Senator Ted Kennedy denounced the battle in the U.S. Senate, and the U.S. public, which had accepted American casualties as the cost of defeating Communism, now saw it as a waste of life. In 1969, 11,780 U.S. military personnel died in the war. By April 1969, the number of U.S. troops in Vietnam was at its highest with around 543,400 men and women. President Richard Nixon would eventually decree that going forward, it would be the South Vietnamese doing the fighting, and U.S. troops would be doing the withdrawing.

I had not left Vietnam, though, and yes indeed, the casualties that we suffered on Hamburger Hill and around the country were bad. In truth, however, very few Vietnam veterans actually fired their weapons. The revisionism accorded to that war by Hollywood made it sound as if we were daily grinding out an action movie, firing our weapons at the Viet Cong with one hundred percent precision when not pulling out grenade pins with our teeth. If you try to pull a pin out of a grenade with your teeth, you will lose your teeth. You used your fingers, which were most likely shaking.

The Vietnamese group that I was advising engaged the enemy a lot, so I saw my share of combat. I had my watch shot off, I had the heel of my boot shot off, and I had a round go through my sleeve. Once I was in a little dent in the ground with two guys on either side of me. Both of them took rounds that went through their foreheads and killed them instantly. The round aimed at me ricocheted off the top of my helmet, which hurt like hell, but I was alive. I don't know how many times enemy soldiers had their guns aimed at my head, but they didn't manage to get me.

It's very hard to describe what combat is. You get very intuitive. When you hear a boom, you discern if it originates from a crew-served weapon, which means that more than one person is aiming that weapon at you. A .51 caliber North Vietnamese machine gun on wheels is a crew-served weapon and could be on a frontal attack.

So, did I need to begin to maneuver against it? Or did I need to stay put? You have to think quickly and keep your cool as you devise your strategy, which causes enormous anxiety. It's not easy to keep your cool.

So, it takes some experience to get a sense of the enemy's pattern. Are they probing? Are they attacking? If it was 3:00 in the morning, and the whistles started blowing, we knew that they were coming. If we were walking down a path and, suddenly, we received a burst of gunfire, that was more of a firefight. You would wonder, "How serious are they with this attack?" And take it from there. So, you get used to it, but the fear never left me. I was always scared. In April 1969, we saw some action near An Son Village, Binh Duong Province and, because of that action, I was awarded the Vietnamese Medal of Honor. I was also decorated twice by the U.S. for heroism. There are only four Army decorations for combat, and one is a Bronze Star with V for heroism. You receive it for ground combat, and then they put oak leaf clusters on it to mark the second decoration you receive. I also have a Combat Infantry Badge, which says that, at this date at these coordinates, this man was in ground combat against a hostile force. It's the Army saying that I really was there.

HEADQUARTERS
UNITED STATES MILITARY ASSISTANCE COMMAND, VIETNAM
APO San Francisco 96222
GENERAL ORDERS 16 June 1969
NUMBER 3254

AWARD OF THE BRONZE STAR MEDAL (FIRST OAK LEAF CLUSTER)

1. TC 320. The following AWARD is announced.
WARDELL, CHARLES W. B. III 05261370 (SSAN 071-33-1376) 1ST ARMOR USA

Awarded: Bronze Star Medal (First Oak Leaf Cluster) with "V" Device
Date action: 3 April 1969
Theater: Republic of Vietnam

Reason: For heroism in connection with military operations against a hostile force: First Lieutenant Wardell distinguished himself by heroic action on 3 April 1969 while serving as Assistant Battalion Advisor, 1st Battalion, 7th Regiment, Fifth Infantry Division, Army of the Republic of Vietnam. On that date in the vicinity of An Son Village, Binh Duong Province, the 1st Battalion was conducting a search and clear operation. During the initial conduct of the operation the lead company encountered light enemy fire from a small bunker complex. After a brief exchange fire the enemy withdrew, and the company began destroying the bunkers. In the process of denying the enemy the use of the bunkers, one Vietnamese soldier stepped on a booby trap. Learning of the casualty, Lieutenant Wardell, who was operating with the battalion command post, volunteered to move forward to direct a medical evacuation of the wounded soldier. With the evacuation helicopter only ten feet off the ground, the perimeter defense began receiving intense enemy fire, Lieutenant Wardell reacted immediately by ordering the helicopter to stop its approach and hold at a safe distance for further instructions. He then advised his counterpart on the deployment of his crew-served weapons to suppress the enemy fire and, exposing himself to intense enemy fire, assisted in the recovery of the wounded soldiers and administered aid. Because of Lieutenant Wardell's suggestions, the company commander gained fire superiority which allowed him the necessary time to reorganize his company for counteraction. The enemy was forced to retreat, and Lieutenant Wardell recalled the medical evacuation helicopter and directed the evacuation of the wounded and dead. First Lieutenant Wardell's heroic actions were in keeping with the highest traditions of the United States Army and reflect great credit upon himself and the military service.

Authority: By direction of the President under the provisions of Executive Order 11046, 24 August 1962.

I got the medals and felt honored, and I still feel honored, but it came with a lot of loss, grief, and death. I've always thought that one of the reasons there are so many missing in action, or MIAs, in Vietnam is that, if you were killed in action, your family received $10,000.

Come Up Big

Your family then had thirty days to clear post or move out of military housing. If you were declared MIA, then you were promoted in rank and legally declared dead seven years later during which time your family could live on post. And so, a lot of guys said, "Hey, you know if I get waxed over here, write to my wife, and tell her I'm dead, but if you can, put me down for MIA because it makes life a hell of a lot easier for my family back home." I have no way of knowing if that was accurate, but it's what I thought.

The other reason for the MIAs is simply due to the type of war we were fighting. America has a great and noble tradition of not abandoning our dead. However, when you're in a heavy triple canopy jungle with dense vegetation around you and treetops blocking out most of the sunlight and the temperatures hitting 100-plus Fahrenheit, and it's damp and dark and wet, it was impossible to carry out dead bodies. So, while we wanted with every ounce of our being to bring our dead out, the environment in which we operated made that wish one that seldom, if ever, came true. It's one of the things you have to live with, leaving the dead behind. It's not easy.

I was once near the Cambodian border in the fishhook area of Vietnam on a mountain near another mountain called the "Black Virgin." The 5th ARVN unit I was with "captured" a North Vietnamese woman. We all took great pleasure in thinking that her unexpected surrender was part of the Americans' propaganda program which was aimed at the North Vietnamese to convince them to come over to the side of democracy. It turned out that we didn't capture her at all but that she voluntarily came across the line waving a white flag because she was being sexually abused by her battalion commander, and she had just grown tired of it. She had decided to come over to the other side to get away from him.

Not only did it show how bad leaders can drive people literally into the hands of their declared enemies but also revealed how frail and almost fraudulent the American propaganda programs were. The U.S. effort to convince the Communists that a better life awaited them in our world was completely sincere, but the North Vietnamese shut it down completely.

Many don't realize that North Vietnamese troops traveled along the battle route with political officers by their sides or, at least, nearby. The typical North Vietnamese arrangement was this: the enemy had the frontline troops, then they had political officers, and then they had the commanding structure in the rear. If you were part of the frontline troops, you were either going to get shot going forward or get shot coming back by the political officers, but you weren't leaving alive of your own free will.

So, the world that the North Vietnamese faced as they came South was highly political. They never believed a word that came out of South Vietnam. We would go to villages and secure them from the North, and then we would leave. The South Vietnamese were incredulous. "You're leaving?" the villagers would ask us. "We'll be back," we'd say. But the villagers were very right to be skeptical of us, and the North Vietnamese re-enforced their doubts.

We honestly tried to implement the many things that the United States had tried to bring to Vietnam, but because we didn't have any stark geographic boundaries the way that armies did in World War I and World War II, we were always swimming in the swamp. We were trying to chase away the North Vietnamese instead of taking territory and establishing our vision of things. We could be in a village one day and not come back for two years. So, it made the mission very confusing, and one of the hallmarks of good leadership is clarity of purpose. This is what the mission is, and this is how we need to do it. We did not have clarity in Vietnam.

The irony of our battle in Vietnam is that there was no "there" there. We had no boundaries. The landscape melted into itself, so we weren't ever really sure where we were. We could have been advancing toward a force that we didn't know was there. Pulling back was not as you might think because we weren't pulling off a line. We weren't pulling away from anything. We were just moving.

We were all using French maps, as well, so nobody really knew where they were. If you got lost, you'd call in to the operation's firebase. And then you'd tell the operator, "You need to send me a white phosphorus shell because I think I'm in this neighborhood, so send a shell out to these coordinates. And I'll see if I can find it." Then we'd get someone to climb a tree to look to see if he could see the damn shell.

This caused two problems. If you didn't see the phosphorus shell explode, you were really lost. And if you gave the firebase your exact coordinates, the shell would come down upon your head. It seems absurd in today's GPS world. We had been asked to defeat Communism. For most of the time, though, we didn't know where the hell we were. It kind of sums up the war.

The other failure of leadership I witnessed came during a "psyops" event, which refers to psychological operations used by the military to influence the enemy through nonviolent means such as dropping leaflets urging surrender and so on. The 5th ARVN had cornered three North Vietnamese soldiers in a cave, but they were alive. The grizzled veterans stood to the side of the cave, not in front of it, because we knew that the three cavemen could shoot us dead. The American command, knowing that we had three live North Vietnamese soldiers trapped, insisted on sending out a psyops officer. A young American major came out and alighted from his helicopter, wearing his brand-new uniform and carrying a megaphone. I suggested to him that he might want to stand on the side of the cave because these were really bad guys in this small cave.

But he stood in front of the cave, and he started speaking his Vietnamese to tell them that he had pamphlets that he would like them to read that would change their ways and, boom, they blew his head off. They put a round right through the megaphone, which went right through his head. So, we threw grenades into the cave, and that was that. It was, however, a sadly stark example of a so-called leader showing up with an agenda that he refused to connect to the reality around him.

In May 1969, I was summoned to headquarters and met with Colonel Leach who, like many senior American officers in Vietnam, had served in World War II. He told me that I had been selected to be the executive officer in Lam Son for the U.S. Adviser Group with the 5th Armored Division.

This was a highly coveted assignment by guys like me who had already done six or seven months in the field, to be brought out of the field to be the executive officer of the 5th ARVN Advisor Group for the remaining months we had left. It was a genuinely nice bump up.

That was the second building block for me in my own journey to leadership. You didn't get that promotion by doing a shitty job in the field. Once again, the Army had noticed something in me that my various schools to date had not seen. It was an unbelievable professional win for me because every young officer wanted to be the executive officer advising the Vietnamese, and now I was going to be that guy.

In fact, after I had returned to the U.S. and was safely home in Cold Spring Harbor, I received a very flattering letter from the Army asking me to please come back. It said that I could become a general officer and that they would like me to make a career out of the military. I said no thanks.

We really tried like hell to help the South Vietnamese people. We really tried to win their hearts and minds. From where I saw the country, we had made a superhuman effort in Vietnam to serve our president, to serve our country, and do what we were being asked to do.

We trained the Vietnamese to fight like us. And that's fighting with an abundance of ammunition, an abundance of food, an abundance of weapons, airplanes, and artillery. We tried to train them to fight like we fought World War II with a sophisticated supply chain of weapons and military tactics that made the best of artillery and air cover before a ground assault.

However, as we started to withdraw from the country, we left them without anything. These Vietnamese officers kept asking us over and over again, "You're not leaving, are you?" or those who accepted that we were going would say, "You can't leave us like this." So, as we began to pull out but were still with the South Vietnamese, it occurred to me that we were eventually going to leave them high and dry, which in turn would make them want to fight less and less. And, of course, that's exactly what happened.

One of the problems with the Vietnam experience was there was great inequality from a soldier's point of view in every aspect. Some people, like Dick Cheney, got deferred five times. He told a reporter in 1989 that "I had other priorities in the '60s than military service." The people who were fighting also had other priorities, like staying alive, but they did not have deferments. We were there fighting for our nation. But knowing that anybody who had the resources to dodge having to fight in Vietnam did so was demoralizing to those of us who went there and served. It suggested pretty clearly that there were two classes of existence in the United States. Those who served the country when they were called upon and those who would find a way to escape that service and who were not called out for dodging it.

The other problem for us in Vietnam (and, yes, in

addition to all the rest) was that President Lyndon Johnson, along with Congress, never officially declared it to be a war. So, it was like the Korean "War," which was a war without officially being declared one, and it killed 37,000 Americans from 1950–1953. That meant the benefits paid out by the U.S. government to returning soldiers from Vietnam were different and less than those paid out to World War II veterans. We even had to have a special act of Congress passed just to get our medals because we weren't fighting in a declared war.

We had been ordered to go overseas to fight against a sophisticated ground force for a government that wouldn't declare war that also had a deferment system for those who were "otherwise engaged." That was blatantly not equal. As well as this: the people we were fighting with, the South Vietnamese, had been fighting against the North Vietnamese and Communists for many years. The South Vietnamese army was very wary of our involvement, and, in fact, I was told many times that they didn't want us there. They were not alone.

Before I left, I was in a firefight that was beginning to heat up quite rapidly. One of our guys, a South Vietnamese soldier, was operating the M60 machine gun, which was always the first target on which the enemy focused. The enemy, in general, would focus on taking out automatic weapons.

We were taking a lot of enemy fire, and I was going up and down the line telling the South Vietnamese to shoot lower and to hit somebody. To this day, one of my lasting characteristics born of that war is that the bigger the problem I face, the lower the voice I use. So, I wasn't screaming at anyone. I was just being matter of fact—or as matter of fact as I could be while being shot at.

The South Vietnamese soldier looked up at me and he said, "Lieutenant, I'm getting the fuck out of here." And I said, "We'll be right behind you." Sometimes that time-honored military strategy of retreating to survive is the best one.

Of course, what we were asked to do had changed in the year that I had been in Vietnam. When President Richard Nixon took his oath of office in January 1969, he knew that he had to end the war. "Peace with honor," they called it. Even so, he ramped up bombing campaigns on the North Vietnamese to pressure them to come to the negotiating table. At the same time, Nixon began withdrawing U.S. forces in June 1969 and, from then on, the U.S. troop withdrawal continued. The U.S. strategy was something known as "Vietnamization" in which we tried to help the South Vietnamese build the combat capability and leadership to face the North Vietnamese without us because we were leaving.

It's a shame that it's all been discredited because, at that point, the American military was at its absolute best. We were good fighters. And the North Vietnamese knew it. We knew it. The military knew it, as well, and we were never defeated in the field. But we were defeated politically, for sure. Our leaders, politically, and some in the field let us down. And all of the Vietnamese knew this.

The South Vietnamese Army had been fighting forever, and it was crooked and political. It was built on connections. The senior management leadership was very connected to its general. So, you were tied to it whether that horse came in or not.

The enlisted men were just exhausted. They'd been doing this forever. They didn't care. There was no NCO leadership even though we tried to build that. The officers lived in beautiful conditions, and the enlisted men did the fighting in the swamps. After a good long while at it, nobody wanted to fight.

One of the blessings of my tour was that the enemy probably paid off the commanding general (or he paid them) of the 5th ARVN division. So, for example, during the Tet Offensive of 1968, the 5th ARVN was the one place that didn't get hit by the North Vietnamese.

In May 1969, I went back to Lam Son to be the executive officer. I was going to come home in October, so all I had to do was hang on for five months. I was relieved but, in the back of my mind, I always had the feeling that something could happen to change the plan. It did. In September, I was told that I was going back to the field.

It was more than a shock. I had been dealing with executive officer stuff, not combat stuff—and now, with a little over a month left in my tour, I was being sent back into the field to face the enemy. Not only that, but I was going on a crazy kind of mission. The kind that gets guys killed.

I was going to do reconnaissance on a road that was re-opening that hadn't been used since 1964. The French had built this fifty-four-mile, two-lane road north to Laos in the 1950s, and it led up through the fishhook area of Vietnam, straight into Communist territory. I was going to do the reconnaissance with the Vietnamese soldiers up this deserted road. I mean, I couldn't say "No!" and I was terrified.

To this day, I still dream about Vietnam. Not about being in combat but about being sent back. And I think, "Isn't that war ever going to end?" and "Do I really have to do all that again?" A lot of it has to do with the end of my tour of duty.

That's what I was thinking at the time—that this war, for me, was never going to end. I was told to report to an American Army unit, the 11th Armored Cavalry Regiment, which was going to travel up that lonely road with us because they gave us real firepower in case all hell rained down. So, I reported to this gung-ho American unit, and I felt like a third string quarterback who was sitting on a bench during a game that was beyond reach, saying to myself, "Don't look at me coach... Don't look at me... I don't want to play."

I saluted the officer who just happened to be Colonel George S. Patton IV, the son of the famous World War II general. He had his father's ivory handled pistol and that same swagger. He just looked at me and said, "You've been highly recommended, son. You're going to be out in front of us. If you need any help, you just get on the horn."

I said, "Thank you, sir." I was pretty much on my own. Again.

Patton had tracks on armored personnel carriers plus light tanks to make it up this road for those who were driving it, but I was walking. And so, we moved out. We were in the jungle, surrounded by the enemy. I was beginning to get a very severe nervous twitch, and I was very thin. I figured that, right about now, I was at the end of the line.

We opened that road for the first time in five years. And it, in a way, was the worst aspect of war because the North Vietnamese had surrounded us. We anticipated a real fight, but it never happened. The thinking was that the enemy wanted the road opened as well, to improve their own supply line. But I wasn't thinking that at all. I was really a nervous wreck. You get your map out and look at it and say, "If we go around this bend, it's a perfect ambush. So, let's go this way, because they may not anticipate that."

They were there, and they let us know they were there, but they never attacked us. We made it all the way up the road to the town of Dong Ha, and then we turned around and came back down. I never fired a shot, but I was terrified the whole time. It's difficult to describe the rhythm of war: the intense periods of combat, the long periods of boredom, and the periods in between along with the constant fear. You have to keep doing it and keep doing it. But, eventually, my time in Vietnam was up. I was going home.

The Army sent me off with one more commendation, and this one is my proudest as it was given to me by my peers:

THE ARMY COMMENDATION MEDAL
Is presented to
FIRST LIEUTENANT CHARLES W.B.

Charles W. B. Wardell III

WARDELL III
United States Army

For distinguishing himself by meritorious service during the period October 1968 to September 1969 while serving as Assistant Battalion Advisor, 1st Battalion, 7th Regiment, 5th Infantry Division, Army of the Republic of Vietnam, and later as Assistant Commander, Headquarters Detachment, Advisory Team 70, United States Army Advisory Group, III Corps Tactical Zone, United States Military Assistance Command, Vietnam. During his tenure with the 1st Battalion, 7th Regiment, Lieutenant WARDELL exhibited an extraordinary degree of professional knowledge, aggressiveness, competence, and leadership rarely found among junior officers in a combat environment. In his latter assignment, Lieutenant WARDELL again displayed high professional competence and organizational skills enabling him to accomplish each task assigned to him in an outstanding manner. Lieutenant WARDELL'S devotion to duty, courage under fire, and professional attitude earned him the highest admiration and respect of all with whom he served. First Lieutenant WARDELL'S performance of duty was in keeping with the highest traditions of the United States Army and reflects great credit upon himself and the military service.

Then I came home to a life I had left, one that had

Come Up Big

sent me to Vietnam. Now I had to connect with it again—
to see if I could change it for the better.

Charles W. B. Wardell III

That's me as a toddler, with all my life ahead of me.

My first Jeep! Little did I know as I played in that beloved vehicle I would one day wind up in the Jeeps of War.

This is me with my mother and my dog Terry.

My grandparents' house in Bay Ridge, Brooklyn, NY. They weren't rich, but it was a nice house.

My father Charles, doing his duty in the South Pacific in World War II.

My family home in Cold Spring Harbor, New York, a modest, rambling, fun place to grow up.

I am at the back, far right, at the East Woods School. I was always on the edge of things, until I went into the Army.

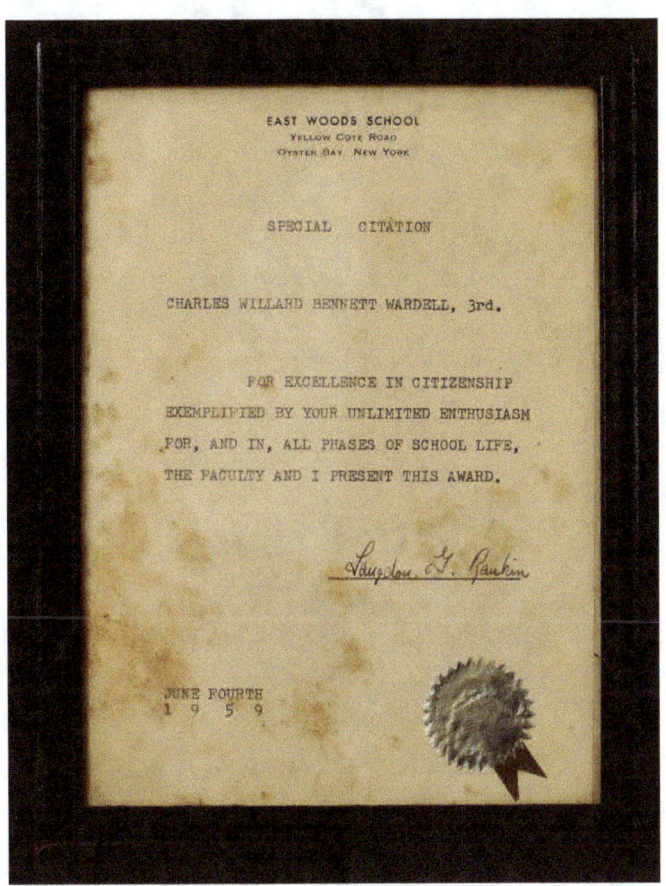

My first award comes to me from the East Woods School, given to me out of sympathy, I suspect.

Come Up Big

I loved hockey, and I loved playing it for my high school, Taft.

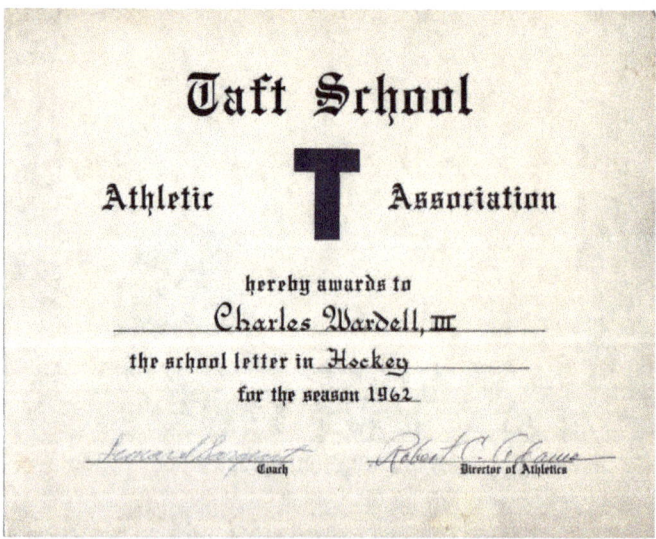

I wasn't too bad at hockey. I lettered in the sport at Taft in 1962 and 1963.

That's Dwight Miller (front left), my best friend from childhood, and me (second right) on the ship to France when I was in high school. We were thinking of French wine and French beaches.

That's me enjoying the South of France on the high school trip I made with Dwight.

That's me with my younger brothers Chris and David, and older sister Wendy.

Me as a freshman at Hamilton College in my dorm room. The wary look is real.

I got accepted into Hamilton College to play hockey, so that's what I did.

Me and Jean Louis, my French passenger, on the road in 1965, the year I drove him across America, sampling some local beverages.

My first Army posting, at Fort Lewis, Washington, Autumn 1966.

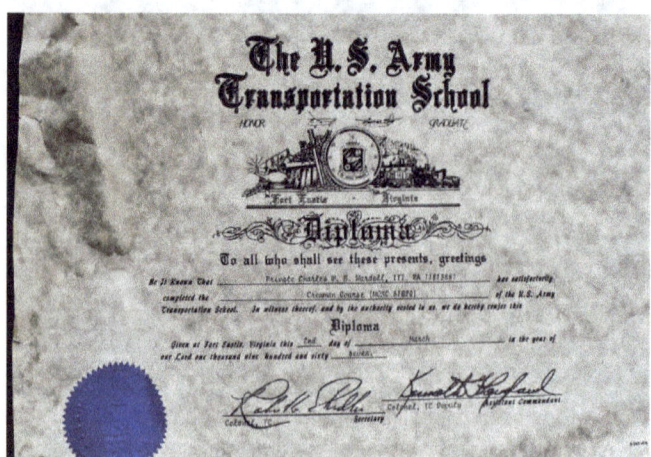

My Army Transportation School diploma. I was an Honors Graduate, and it gave me a real shot of pride. I never expected such success would come to me in the Army.

My U.S. Army commission as a 2nd Lieutenant, November 2, 1967.

Me as 2nd Lieutenant, with no idea what was ahead of me.

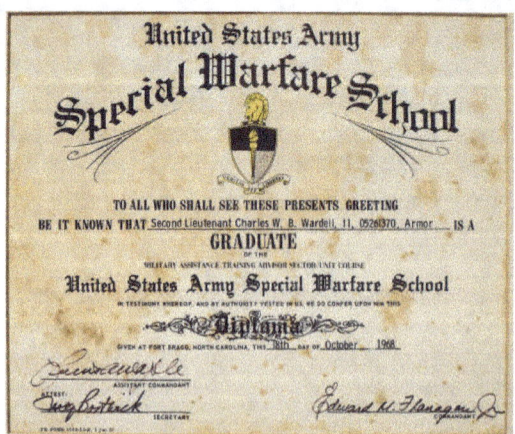
My Special Warfare Diploma.

Getting my Bronze Star, in late Spring 1969, in Vietnam.

Me and Major Dinh, my Vietnamese counterpart whom I respected a lot.

HEADQUARTERS
UNITED STATES MILITARY ASSISTANCE COMMAND, VIETNAM
APO San Francisco 96222

GENERAL ORDERS
NUMBER 3254

16 June 1969

AWARD OF THE BRONZE STAR MEDAL
(FIRST OAK LEAF CLUSTER)

1. TC 320. The following AWARD is announced.

WARDELL, CHARLES W. B. III   05261370   (SSAN 071-33-1376)   1LT ARMOR USA
Awarded: Bronze Star Medal (First Oak Leaf Cluster) with "V" Device
Date action: 3 April 1969
Theater: Republic of Vietnam
Reason: For heroism in connection with military operations against a hostile force: First Lieutenant Wardell distinguished himself by heroic action on 3 April 1969 while serving as Assistant Battalion Advisor, 1st Battalion, 7th Regiment, 5th Infantry Division, Army of the Republic of Vietnam. On that date in the vicinity of An Son Village, Binh Duong Province, the 1st Battalion was conducting a search and clear operation. During the initial conduct of the operation the lead company encountered light enemy fire from a small bunker complex. After a brief exchange fire the enemy withdrew, and the company began destroying the bunkers. In the process of denying the enemy the use of the bunkers, one Vietnamese soldier stepped on a booby trap. Learning of the casualty, Lieutenant Wardell, who was operating with the battalion command post, volunteered to move forward to direct a medical evacuation of the wounded soldier. With the evacuation helicopter only ten feet of the ground, the perimeter defense began receiving intense enemy fire. Lieutenant Wardell reacted immediately by ordering the helicopter to stop its approach and hold at a safe distance for further instructions. He then advised his counterpart on the deployment of his crew-served weapons to suppress the enemy fire and, exposing himself to intense enemy fire, assisted in the recovery of the wounded soldiers and administered aid. Because of Lieutenant Wardell's suggestions, the company commander gained fire superiority which allowed him the necessary time to reorganize his company for counteraction. The enemy was forced to retreat, and Lieutenant Wardell recalled the medical evacuation helicopter and directed the evacuation of the wounded and dead. First Lieutenant Wardell's heroic actions were in keeping with the highest traditions of the United States Army and reflect great credit upon himself and the military service.
Authority: By direction of the President under the provisions of Executive Order 11046, 24 August 1962

My official Bronze Star Award for "heroic action" on
April 3, 1969.

Me in Vietnam. Middle image right is Major Dinh with his family, who traveled with us as we waged war.

Come Up Big

Headquarters
5th Infantry Division Advisory Detachment
Advisory Team 70, APO 96314
Lam Son, Vietnam

MACOZ-III-5   6 January 1969

SUBJECT: Letter of Congratulations

1LT Charles W.B. Wardell, III
Asst Bn Adv
1st Bn, 7th Regt
Advisory Team 70
APO 96314

1. I congratulate you on your being awarded the Combat Infantryman Badge. Your performance under hostile fire truly indicates that you deserve to wear this distinguished award, worn with pride by U.S. combat infantrymen around the world.

2. Keep up the good work.

JAMES H. LEACH
Colonel, Armor
Senior Advisor

My Combat Infantry Badge.

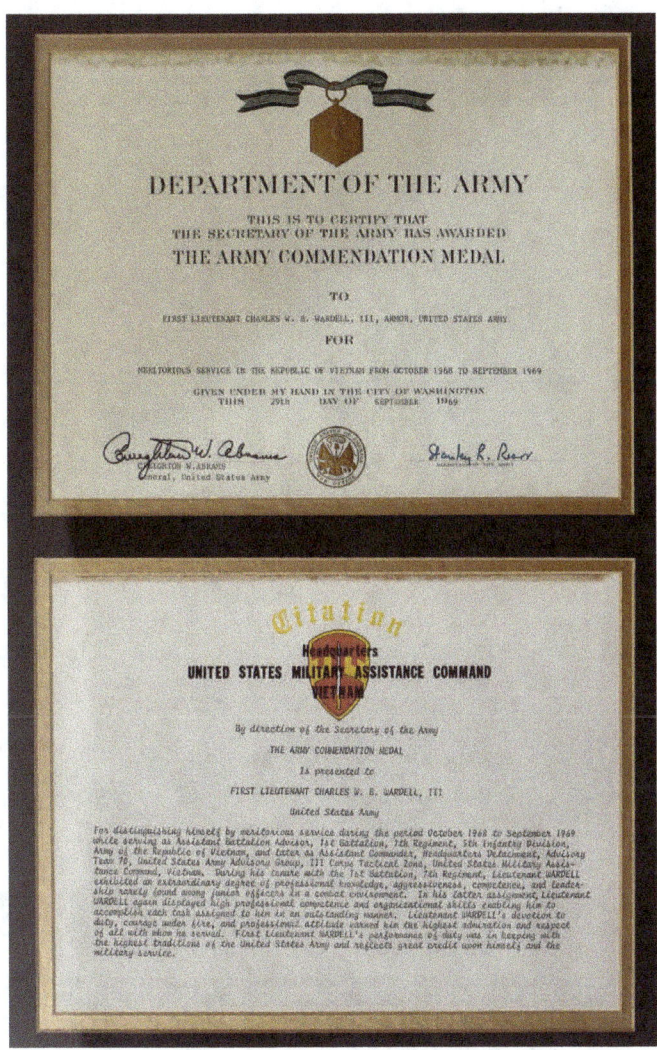

My Army Commendation Medal for my year at war.

Me in Vietnam (top) and me at home, my first night back from the war. Smiling with relief, and with apprehension. What would I do next?

Charles W. B. Wardell III

Dear Ma and Dad,
   I'm not nearly as tired as I was the last time I wrote. I didn't want to worry you, but I just can't keep all that to myself. I find I get extremely depressed and I really don't know what to do. I really can't get along with my "Capt." and the living conditions, weather, bugs, dirt take some getting used to. After Sat my nerves are rough to control. On our

last operation we went back to the same place. All the men just sat around, not slept, etc and I kept trying to put out security etc but no one seemed at all interested. We are going to build the Compound but I don't think it will be too bad. VC is too easy to avoid and not important enough for Charlie to pay the price. Hopefully. So far I haven't gotten any mail, but I

we can't put it up as often as I'd like. I hope the address I'm giving is correct. I can't think of anything I might need, except a break at the Paris Talks. I said I was looking forward to Vietnam and now I'd love to come home for a cold beer.

My best to everyone and the boys at Fitt.
Dick

Here's the original letter I sent to my parents from Vietnam. I know they laughed about me loving a cold beer. But they did indeed have a cold beer waiting for me when I got home. I took it as proof of their love and finally their pride in their first-born son.

Chapter 5
"The miracle bounce."

When it was time for me to leave Vietnam and go home, the 1969 World Series was in play. In the first National League Championship Series, the New York Mets had swept the favored Atlanta Braves in three games. I was rotated out through Saigon, and I remember listening to the Braves and Mets on the radio. They were playing a baseball game back home, and I was so far away in a war zone, preparing to go back to the land where an American game could overtake the reality of an American war in the public imagination. It was a surreal contrast.

I spent a night in Saigon. And, the next day, wearing my jungle fatigues, I got an airplane and flew back to the Oakland Army terminal. I returned home as I had departed—by myself. At the Oakland Army terminal, I had a physical examination and received a fresh uniform of dress blues, and they helped me to get a TWA ticket to John F. Kennedy Airport. Then I was on my way back to New York.

My mother and my two younger brothers met me at the airport. In those days, before intense airport security, you could walk to the plane doorway when you were meeting someone. I saw my brothers, and I said by way of greeting them, "You fuckers!" To this day, they don't know why I said that. But that was an endearment in my world of war. We would say it to one another after an enemy engagement. "You fuckers!" You made it. You're alive.

I went home. I was back in our house in Cold Spring Harbor and back in my old room. My family was happy to have me home and proud of it. It was no longer "Oh, Chuck, too bad he's such a nice guy..." to a new he-can-do anything order—or almost.

Happiness for me was seeing my beloved golden lab, Terry. For the first time in his dog life he came upstairs and slept on my bed the night before I left for Vietnam. Then he died within a few days of my return. It was as if that dog had just been waiting to see me home safe and sound. It was very sad to see my grand old golden lab wait for me and then die.

But I hung on to my past and my memories. I put on a camouflage uniform as that's what I had been wearing all the time for the past year. And I just sat there. I was once again Chucky Wardell, and I was twenty-four years old. I hadn't graduated from college, and I had no plans. While my family saw their oldest boy back safe and sound, I saw a gloomy and troubled future.

I also had a real burden to carry from my time at war and, as PTSD was not a thing then, I just saw it as the rock around my neck. I only had one thing to talk about, and that was Vietnam. I bored my family and my friends to death. I was trying to get back to my life as a civilian, which had been in disruption before I left, but I had a hard time leaving the jungle war.

When I came home from Vietnam, I had no fellow travelers to share my experiences with. None of my friends had gone to Vietnam. Those who served had done so in the Navy like my friend Dwight Miller. None of them saw combat, and they weren't draftees. I was drafted. I went. I saw combat. And I didnt resent that. When I got asked to leave Hamilton, I was starting all over again when I came home. Now, I was coming home from war without any job or anything else waiting for me. Once again, I had to start all over.

I also knew that I had learned things. I had led men under very difficult conditions, and I was good at it. The Army had made me realize that I was not some stupid ice hockey player but a guy with skills, talent, and intelligence.

It was a huge realization at that point in my life because not only had I survived the war, but I had also come out stronger. I knew I would survive whatever happened next, as well.

Even so, my overwhelming sense of coming home was one of guilt. I felt that I really didn't do as well as I could have done in Vietnam. My peers had judged me to be a highly successful combat officer. But I didn't judge myself that way, and the sense that I could have done more was like a hangover from my college days when I did not succeed no matter what I tried. Failure still haunted me, which is one of the aspects of PTSD, and which I did not know at the time. One of the lasting emotions I have of the Vietnam era in my life is guilt. Which is not unusual, but it's very real.

And then, suddenly, I had been sent away from that war, and I was sitting all alone in my childhood room. It reminded me of somebody who suddenly had everybody else in their entire family killed in an airplane crash, and they had survived because they were the one person who didn't get on the plane. You were truly by yourself.

One of the ironies of it all is that I had a friend, John Rowe, who was in the 173rd Airborne and he was really upset that he had received compassionate emergency leave to come home because a family member of his was dying and so he had missed the big fight on Hamburger Hill. His sister Pam told me that he regretted not being there. He had come home before a third of his company were killed. It was counterintuitive: we should be relieved and grateful. But no, we are not. We now at least have a term for it: survivor's guilt. And John died with that guilt.

Mine wasn't so much survivor's guilt because I had plenty of chances not to be a survivor. It was the guilt of asking people to do things that killed or wounded them. It was wheels within wheels. So, depression and guilt came home with me. At the end of World War II, American soldiers came home to ticker tape parades and were celebrated as heroes who had defeated evil. When I came home from Vietnam, there were no parades, and more than a few people regarded me as evil for having participated in a war that was now deeply opposed in the United States. The country, and indeed the world, had taken sides and, for many people, I had been on the wrong side of history. I didn't even say I had been in the service unless I could trust my environment completely. And I couldn't quite do that yet outside of my family home.

At least I was safe, but I was not so sound. I had developed a bad nervous facial twitch and was twitching almost uncontrollably in my face and in my eyes. So, in the fall of 1969, I was at home and thinking, "What the hell am I going to do here?" The military wanted me to come back and make a career of it. I'd been a very good soldier and had been highly rated in my efficiency reports. But I was never going back to the military. My job had been to ask people to do things in the field for their country, and then some of them would wind up dead because of my ask. I couldn't do that anymore.

I really thought about getting psychological help, but that's all I did, and I did not follow up by going to see anyone. My parents were hardworking, and they were of the World War II generation where you did your bit for your country and then life went on no matter how much you had suffered. They were proud of my service and, while I talked about it too much, which I regret a bit now, I didn't have much else in my arsenal of life experience to talk about.

There were war protests everywhere, but what I found so discouraging was the day-to-day interaction with people who discounted me because I'd been fighting in Vietnam. Friends, college administrators, and women who wouldn't date me all showed total disgust that, in many ways, made me feel like I did when I was asked to leave Hamilton. In my mind, I had done everything I could to answer what my country asked me to do without being a martyr. I had survived combat and proven myself while engaging an enemy. One of the things about being a veteran is living with everybody else's exaggerations. I have heard story after bullshit story from veterans that I know are completely false. In a society that gave no credit to any of it, true or false, it was hard to bear.

My peers just thought, "Yeah, Chuck, you ended up down on the ground in Vietnam because you flunked out of school." It wasn't like going to town and saying that I had just become a partner at a major law firm. I was saying that I survived a terrible war in Vietnam because, even though I flunked out of college, I somehow made it through the battle.

Once, at a party, a friend of my father's was trying to be nice to me and suggested that I become a truck driver as he said that he could help me to get a job behind the wheel of any delivery truck that I wanted. I think that was the nadir of any hope I had of being successful on the terms I now imagined.

Nonetheless, I thought I had better get a job to stay sane and make some money. I saw a help wanted sign and answered it, and I got the job. I started working in Knutson's shipyard in Huntington, Long Island for $2 an hour. Which was $16 a day or $12 a day after taxes and that put $60 a week in my pocket (which is about $500 a week today).

It was an awkward time in my life socially as well. I tried to date women back home as I had now become a man of the world in the rest and relaxation spots of the Vietnam war, and I wanted female companionship. There were more than a few instances where fathers of women I was interested in would call my family and yell, "We don't want our daughter going out with your son, period!"—then slam the phone down. Some guy came over to my father in the Huntington Country Club dining room and started screaming at him about my service in Vietnam. How could he have even let me come back into his house?

My father stood up, then pointed at him and said with a kind of calm ferocity, "You're a traitor." The dining room went dead silent. My family was very proud of me. I had served my country, I had been decorated, and I had returned home to continue my life. So, that's what I had to do, pick up at the place where I left off even if that seemed like it might be the most challenging place to begin again.

I also applied to colleges to see if, after my war experience, if there was some other academy that would see what the Army had seen in me. My mother and I went out to Southampton Community College at the end of Long Island, and I had an interview with them. After my interview, the dean sidled up to my mother and said, "I don't think he is a fit. We're not going to take him. So don't make us turn him down." The interviewer had basically told my mother that they did not want a Vietnam vet, like me, to be present on their august campus.

The most embarrassing incident happened when I went to Brown University, and I was sitting in the admissions waiting room, about to go on a tour of the campus with kids who were eighteen years old. The director of admissions came out and told me right in front of everyone that they were not even going to give me a tour. In fact, he said, "Why don't you just go home?" They did not want a former Army officer on their campus, either.

The calendar landed in December 1969. Since I had attended the Taft School, my father called them in quasi desperation to see if they could help me to find a way out. I went up to visit them, about one hundred miles to the north, in Watertown, Connecticut. I had graduated from Taft in 1963. Now it was six years later, and I was going back to my old high school asking for their help.

There was a wonderful dean at Taft, a teacher named Mr. Sullivan, who taught a very tough English course. He said that he would be very happy to help me find a way into college. I had, in the meantime, contacted Hamilton College to ask if they would take me back, and they said no.

So, my mother, not one to take "No" for an answer, wrote Hamilton a letter basically scolding them. "How dare you refuse to take this young man back?" she asked. They responded and then they relented, finally saying, "Chuck Wardell is eligible for readmission." Hamilton also sent a cover letter with that letter that said, "We agree with his decision to seek his education elsewhere," but that didn't matter at all. The "eligible for readmission" letter was all I needed to apply to other colleges as a transfer. You needed to prove, if you wished to transfer colleges, that the place you were leaving would have taken you back. That was the beginning of hope. I thought that I had a chance to transfer into some college somewhere and not be stuck at the shipyard for the rest of my life.

But I kept working in the shipyard to give myself some cash while I kept applying to colleges. I applied to the University of Ohio in Miami and to Ohio Wesleyan. I applied to the Universities of Kentucky, Tennessee, and Florida. I applied to Boston College, the University of

Delaware, and Hofstra. I can't remember all of them, but I applied to a lot of them. And I didn't get into any of them.

So, Mr. Sullivan at Taft, the English teacher who was one of the few academics who said that I was "a really bright guy" said, "We just haven't unlocked him yet," and called Harvard. It was at a time when admissions were more personal and not based on AP boxes ticked off and test scores and GPAs, all swirled around in algorithmic magic potions, which would be fine if we had a national educational standard, but we do not. In any case, Bradley Howe was a Harvard admissions officer and said to Mr. Sullivan, "Okay, if you recommend him, we'll interview him."

Now, that was a little bit of a step up because Harvard, statistically, was just as hard to get into then as it is to get into now, algorithms be damned.

I went to see Bradley, and I had an interview with him. He said, "Look, before we start anything, you have to prove that you can pass something."

I was twenty-four years old, sitting in the Harvard admissions office and being told I had to pass something to prove that I could do the academic work. I was back to square one. I couldn't get into any academic place to "pass something." So, Bradley suggested that I go to Columbia General Studies, which offered adult education, and pass a course there and prove that I was good at something "collegiate" and so, worthy of Harvard's future attention.

I had no chance to get into Harvard—and I was the first in line to subscribe to that theory. Even so, in the spring of 1970, I attended Columbia General Studies, taking an English course as well as a history course. Just before my finals, the Nixon administration invaded Cambodia, and there was a huge public outcry. The colleges went nuts, and everybody at the college quit working in protest.

I was in a jam. I had to apply to the colleges that I had selected as a transfer student. The whole point of doing these two classes at Columbia was to show these colleges, Harvard included, that I could make the cut. But now with this chaos, I couldn't find my professors because there were no classes and no grades. They had vanished.

Once again, I was in the middle of a war drama, one preventing me from getting my hands on a grade to get into a college, any college. I had these two professors who lived in Morningside Heights, which is a neighborhood near Columbia University, but they weren't coming to class. How was I going to get a grade from them to make my future a happy one? So, I badgered the admin to tell me their home addresses which they didn't want to do. But I kept on them and eventually, they coughed them up.

So I ran to Morningside Heights and finally found both gentlemen at their homes.

I knocked on their doors, and I said to them both, "I'm in your class," and they looked at me like I was from Mars. I said to the English prof, "Here's a postcard pre-signed to the Harvard admissions office. I need a grade in my English course," and he put an A on it. The history prof said, "Good luck with that," and he put an A on my card as well. So, I sent the postcard to Harvard with an A in English and an A in American history. I also sent them to Boston University. I was pretty sure I'd get into BU as I'd been told that I was a strong candidate there by their admissions people.

I was told to not open the inevitable Harvard rejection letter when it arrived. Transfer students get admitted later because they filled in the regular admissions first and so, in June of 1970, I got two letters: one from Boston University and that rejection letter from Harvard.

The rest of the colleges that I had seen had already turned me down or, ones like Brown, had turfed me out of the building, so this was the end of the line. At the time, I was at the Cold Spring Harbor Beach Club, which is a small local club that everyone belonged to and featured all you needed for a club: a sandy beach and a bar and a place to park your boat. I was standing in the Cold Spring Harbor Beach Club's parking lot with my girlfriend at the time who was brave enough to date me and, later, to marry me. I opened my letter from Boston University, thinking, "Okay, I can go to BU," but I got turned down flat. In the old days, when you got a thin envelope from a college, it meant you had been turned down and a fatter envelope meant you got in because you had to return a card telling them that you were coming.

The Harvard envelope seemed a little fat to me, but I was just going to throw it out. I thought I was really sunk. I was back again at square one with this giant nightmare of finding a college to take me in still in front of me. So far, everybody who had assessed me had convinced themselves that I was not "college material."

Nevertheless, to get it over with, I opened the letter from Harvard. And it said, "You're accepted."

Bradley Howe said, "We had 950 transfer applicants, and we took sixty." And that I was going to be in college for all four undergraduate years because they were giving me credit for the one public speaking course I took at Hamilton, which was the one course I had enjoyed, and that was it. "If you still would like to come to Harvard, please fill out this postcard and send it back as soon as you can."

I was going to drive that damn postcard to Harvard myself. I was terrified that it would get lost in the mail. I felt a little like I had felt when I knew I was going to Vietnam. I thought, "Holy shit, this can't be happening to me, right?" But I thought about it in a very happy way. And it was happening to me. In June 1970, much to my surprise and to my great relief, I was heading for Harvard. This was my miracle bounce. Kicked out of Hamilton and now on my way to Harvard.

I got into Harvard as a freshman beginning the fall of 1970. It was as competitive then as it is now as I was part of the chosen six percent who had been accepted. At twenty-five years old, I was also the oldest freshman at Harvard. In my first week, I was told I had to learn a language. And I said, "Guys, I can't." I had wrestled with all languages all my life, including English, and this would just be setting myself up for failure before I had even started. So, the Harvard people said, "Well, you can go to the Harvard Medical Center and take a test with a psychologist. And if he agrees that you shouldn't take a language, we will waive that requirement."

So, I went to the Harvard Medical Center. The psychologist was a young hippyish guy in a suit, with a black beard, and long hair. He took me into his office for what was normally a three-hour meeting. He saw my record as a combat veteran. The first thing he showed me, after talking to me for fifteen minutes or so, was a Rorschach test, which was introduced about fifty years earlier in 1921 by Swiss psychiatrist Hermann Rorschach. In this test you look at an inkblot and say what you think it looks like. Some psychologists like to use this test to examine personality characteristics and emotional functioning.

So, he showed me an inkblot and asked, "What does that look like to you?" I looked at it. I don't know why I said what I did, but I told him, "Well, it looks like a dead body. And I haven't killed anybody in quite a while, and I kind of miss it."

He stared at me for a while and said, "You know, I'll let you out of that language class. We don't have to go any further. But I really hope that you enjoy Harvard and settle down a little bit, and you might want to get some help." That was the end of my interview. I never saw him again.

My Harvard roommate was a draft dodger. In his junior year at college, he got his physical examination notice. And passing your physical was the first step in getting sent to Vietnam. He decided to go to Canada, and, on the way, somebody had stolen his driver's license. There had been a robbery in Milton, Connecticut in which a police officer was killed, and my roommate's driver's license was recovered at the scene. So, he was chased by the police in Canada and eventually arrested. They put the cuffs on him and brought him back to Oklahoma where he was from.

The FBI had made it clear that, when they finally got him back to the U.S., he had nothing to do with the robbery or with the police officer's murder. So, the court knew that the robbery wasn't the issue. Evading the draft notice was the issue. He got before a judge who had been a general in World War II. And the judge said that this guy had violated the Selective Service Act but, before the judge could send him off to jail, his attorney said he'd love to go into the U.S. Army.

That was fine with the judge, and this Harvard guy was told to report for his physical, which he should have done four years before. So, he reported, and he failed his physical. He never would have been drafted to begin with. Back to Harvard he went to finish his senior year. And he roomed with me. He was a great guy who went on to do a PhD in petroleum engineering. We got along just fine.

Vietnam followed me in other ways. On October 14, 1970, a bomb had exploded in the Center for International Affairs on the third floor of the museum. The bomb was placed in the desk of an Army colonel who was visiting Harvard for independent study. A woman called the Harvard Police to warn them about the bomb, but luckily no one was in the building at the time. There was huge backlash against the Vietnam War at Harvard while I was there, and it was just one more thing to deal with. After a while you began to think that maybe you had done something wrong. One of the problems came from people I call elitist foghorns who had these opinions about which they would never shut up. They thought they had a right to blatantly criticize because they knew better. They didn't know shit. That was half of Harvard when it came to the Vietnam War.

The journalist Teddy White came up to visit James Thomson who had been the China specialist on the staff of the National Security Council in the Johnson administration. In 1966, Thomson resigned in protest of the Vietnam War and then became a lecturer in history at Harvard. He taught a popular course in American-East Asian Relations. In 1972, he was appointed curator of Harvard's Nieman Foundation for Journalism. We were sitting at some big shot's house, and Teddy White got plastered because he loved to drink. Teddy became a good friend but, on that night, what he was saying about Vietnam annoyed me. "What we got to do is stabilize it." I was sitting there thinking, "Yeah, you go there and try to stabilize it." It's like telling the ocean not to have waves. My life, otherwise, at Harvard, was great. I lived in a building called Kirkland House, which was so named because of Reverend John Thornton Kirkland, class of 1789, who was president of Harvard from 1810 to 1828. Kirkland House was one of the seven original residential houses established at the university in 1931.

Kirkland's Hicks House was once the quarters for officers in General Washington's army, and every year at the start of the first term it recognized this with a ceremony on campus. Both students and faculty deans marched behind Revolutionary War-era reenactors who provided musical accompaniment on eighteenth-century instruments like the drum and the fife. I loved the traditions, and I got involved in campus life. I also met my friend Jack McLean, a fellow Vietnam vet who was a couple of years ahead of me at Harvard.

"I first met Chuck in what was probably my junior year, at Harvard, but it might have been before that," Jack McLean recalled. "I was in the dining club at Harvard, called the Owl Club, and I was the first Vietnam veteran to go to Harvard. So, it was a lonely place. And, somewhere along the way, I met Chuck and suggested that he think about joining the club for the same reason I did—because I was living off campus and was older than most of the kids, and he was even older because he's a couple of years older than I am, and so he did."

Indeed, I joined the Owl Club, which was a male-only club that had been around since 1896, but there I needed a bit of help as you just don't show up and pay at the gate as it were. A neighbor to my family back on Long Island, John Campbell, had been a Harvard man, and he had fought in World War II as a navigator in a B-17. He was shot down, and it took him eighteen months, with the help of the French Resistance, to walk out of Germany through France, across the Pyrenees, and into Spain before making his way back to the United States. People thought he was dead, and they had even "buried" him. He's the only guy I know who ever dug up his own tombstone.

He was now a lawyer, a big fan of Harvard, and involved with the college as a committed alum. He agreed with Jack's advice and said to me, "You should join the Owl Club. It's one of the very superior dining clubs at Harvard." He wrote a letter of recommendation for me, and so I became a member. The Owls were really my friend group at Harvard.

Even though Jack McLean and I were both Vietnam veterans, the subject did not come up.

"We never talked about Vietnam much, if at all," Jack McLean recalled. "Our experiences were very different, and it was also at a time when people just didn't talk about it, right? We weren't embraced when we got home. So, Chuck and I didn't talk about it. I mean, nobody talked about it, even people who had been there together, you know. And he was there [in Vietnam] probably a year after I was there. But he was in the Army. I was in the Marine Corps. So, it was like two totally different deals. What we had in common was that we had both served, and that we were two of the thirty kids in the Owl Club."

Jack McLean served with Charlie Company, 1st Battalion, 4th Marines, 3rd Marine Division. Decades later, after years of grappling with the torment of PTSD and the physical effects of his exposure to the defoliant Agent Orange, which has afflicted so many Vietnam veterans, me included, Jack began to reconnect with his fellow Marines and his journey towards recovery. He also wrote two immensely powerful testimonies to his time in Vietnam, and his recovery from PTSD, *Found* and *Loon*. Both are well worth reading.

As I made my way through Harvard and made other friends, it still took me about fifteen years to get over Vietnam. I was a pretty rough character after having spent a year in combat and, to some degree, I can still be triggered by loud and unexpected noises. I also had a chip on my shoulder. I wasn't in combat every day for twenty-four hours a day. But I was in contact with the enemy a lot, and now I had been vilified by my society for doing my duty. It took me a long time to adjust.

Harvard helped me to get over my anxieties by virtue of its supreme indifference to my history. They didn't care even if I'd been the most decorated soldier in American history. After all, they were Harvard. In their eyes, I was a Harvard undergraduate, and that was good enough. I was talking to people from all across the country and around the world from all walks of life, and I was finding a balance in those conversations. This reality helped me to get over a lot of the things swirling inside me from Vietnam.

There's a funny story that starkly illustrates just how it helped, not only philosophically and emotionally, but practically. I was three months into my freshman year and walking into Harvard Yard. As I walked in, John Harvard's statue was on my right, the administration building was on my left and, directly in front of me, there was a willowy blonde female student. I was wearing fatigues and a field jacket and very much giving off the military air. She stopped dead in front of me, this elegant, beautiful, smart, Harvard undergraduate. She looked down at me because she was taller than me, took in my camouflaged self, and then said, "You know, you're never gonna get laid wearing that."

Come Up Big

So, I changed my style. I switched over to blue jeans and a T-shirt almost as fast as I could get home. It was the beginning of my social re-entry.

I wasn't a brilliant student, but I was good enough and, in the stuff I liked, such as history, I was quite good. I started to regain my intellectual confidence that I had tapped into in the Army. And so I began to live my adult life.

"Instead of sitting around drinking beer like the rest of us, Chuck was pretty diligent about his studies," Jack McLean recalled. "I would see him studying in the Owl Club in the middle of the day, and I think that, because of what he had experienced at Hamilton, he was very responsible about his studies at Harvard."

It was a time when gaining all of this was something that I enormously needed. Otherwise, I think I would have been a bitter, angry, resentful Vietnam veteran for the rest of my days. During a pretty intense time of anti-war activity at Harvard, Chase Peterson, the head of admissions, called me. He mentioned that some students felt the admissions department was out of touch with their views and asked if I wanted to join the Harvard interviewing process.

They wanted an older person, and I was in my mid-twenties. The fact I was a Vietnam vet now mattered as they figured I would show up and do the job, so, with no small irony, I was part of the interviewing process for Harvard. My own brother interviewed with one of my team members for Harvard, but he turned us down and went to Princeton. But I enjoyed the job as it connected me with people and made me feel like I was doing something of value in addition to my studies. In many ways, although Harvard would hate to hear it, they treated me the way that the really good leaders in the military did. When I went to a professor and said, "I don't understand this" about some subject, the Harvard answer was, "Okay. What don't you understand?" There wasn't any questioning of my lack of understanding nor belittling me in a "we've been over this forty times" way. They were genuinely trying to help me get it.

It reminds me of when a football coach would ask the quarterback, "What are you seeing out there on the field?" He would ask the question to try to help the quarterback play his best. At Harvard, they basically said the same thing to me. "What are you seeing out there?" And I replied, "Well, I see it this way." They said, "Well, then, pursue it that way." They knew that I was just seeing the problem differently, and they wanted to know how I saw it. We would work out the solution from there, and I was very much part of it. I was included.

I remember one of my greatest accomplishments at Harvard happened when I took a complicated English lit course. Harvard had three-hour final exams in which we wrote answers to the questions by hand in blue books. There was a section of the exam that I just didn't understand at all. They presented the work of certain authors and asked how I saw them, but I didn't recognize any of the authors. I didn't know what the hell the answer to the question was because I didn't understand the question.

But, instead of panicking, I just sat there and thought, "Okay, what are the trends so far from the first two thirds of the exam? I understand those." And I transposed those trends to the work of the authors in the question that I did not understand. I didn't have any idea what the authors had done or who they were, but my technique worked.

I got an A, and, to this day, I still have not gotten over it. I thought myself through to an A during an exam based upon the fact that I finally felt free to write about the world the way I saw it. That taught me much about how leaders can learn from the people whom they lead. Let the people do their work, and they might just surprise you.

At Harvard, I didn't have any professors who were mentors because I wasn't digging into one particular subject, so I just didn't have that kind of deep professor-student relationship. I was doing general studies, and I touched a lot of bases, so I met a lot of fine teachers. John King Fairbank, a professor of history and esteemed Chinese scholar, was warm and honest. To a Harvard student like me who was asking him a question about history, I didn't get a belittling response. He was interested in my question and how I saw the issue at hand.

My most revealing academic story comes from the class of Daniel Moynihan, who was a professor of education and urban politics. He had served as an advisor to John F. Kennedy, and he would later go on to be one of the Democratic Party's senators from New York. I wrote a paper about President Warren G. Harding's economic policy—the biggest paper that I wrote as a student—and it was for his class. Moynihan reviewed it.

Then Moynihan said, "You know, Chuck, I've reviewed your paper. Twenty percent of Harvard College is brilliant, and eighty percent is lucky to get in, and you're in the eighty percent." I took that as a compliment. I thought, "Great. What more can he ask for?" And he never even graded the paper. He just handed it back to me. But I thought, "Good. I'll take the lucky." And I've felt that way ever since.

Of course, Vietnam did not completely leave me while I was at Harvard. Indeed, it was the reason in a very real way that I was admitted to the college in the first place.

I worked as a Harvard tour guide in the summers as I had a small Vietnam Veterans Affairs (VA) students' benefit. Today, the VA pays for everything, but I got $225 a month from them to go to college. Our benefits were so low because President Johnson did not admit that we were fighting a war and never declared it as such. So why would we be paid proper war service benefits? It was disgraceful.

So, I had my $225 a month from my grateful government as well as some money from my parents helping me, and I worked as a tour guide, and I also worked in the admissions office. I took the courses that interested me because my advisor said I would enjoy general studies at my age. So, I had a chance to really see the breadth of Harvard.

In my senior year, I got the chance to see something that very few get the chance to see. I got a look at my own file as I was in the admissions office, and no one minded that I took a look. After reviewing my file, many things became clear to me about why I was at Harvard when not even the most reckless gambler would have taken odds on that being my academic destination.

I was jolted back to a memory of when I first got home from Vietnam, when I was standing in line at Chemical Bank in Cold Spring Harbor to cash a check. And John Campbell, the guy who wrote me my reference for the Owl Club, was behind me. One of my exploits in Vietnam, which resulted in my receiving a Bronze Star with a V for valor, had made the newspaper, and he'd read it. He just slapped me on the back and congratulated me. He could not have been nicer to me. I said, "Thank you, Mr. Campbell." Unbeknownst to me, he had written Harvard a very strong letter about why they should take me as a student. In 1970, the year I was applying to Harvard, John Campbell headed up the Harvard fund, which raised $27 million for Harvard that year, which today is worth $221 million.

I believe that Harvard had 1,300 Vietnam veterans apply to the college that year, and they only took me. I believe that I'm the only graduate of the Special Warfare School who has gone to Harvard. It was thanks to Mr. Campbell, and also Mr. Sullivan at Taft, and a bit of me, too. You might wonder: if I had not served in Vietnam, would I have ever been a student at Harvard? Probably not is the answer because that conversation with Mr. Campbell would never have happened. But, on the other hand, I was a student at Harvard, and they did not ask me to leave. In fact, they even gave me a degree and praised me for it. So that's good enough for me.

My attitude towards it all is part of my wall sitter

mentality, which is an expression I would learn soon from General Alexander Haig. I got a seat on the edge of the room against the wall, but I didn't get to the Harvard Big Table. I wasn't one of the genius students. But, goddamn it, I got in the room. It was a great boost for me, psychologically, after everything that had happened to me in my various academies in the past. Best of all, I realized now that I had learned how to lead myself.

I also realized that I didn't know what I was going to do after college. My father had gone to college with the chairman of Quaker Oats who came from the family who owns Quaker Oats, so he had some influence at the company. I was interviewed by the human resource director at Quaker Oats who was a very nice man. He said, "Well, someday, if you're really lucky, you may make your age." That is, maybe I could make 1000 times my age as an annual salary.

I was twenty-eight. At the time, I thought that, if I ever made close to $30,000 here or anywhere, that's all the money I would ever need. I was telling that story to David Halperin, a Harvard Law student, after playing squash with him. It was in March 1973, a rainy, cold, New England day. David looked at me and he said, "Make your age?" He shook his head. "You should get to the White House. I think General Haig is going to be the next chief of staff. And Watergate is beginning to unfold. They could use you. I'll write to the general."

David had served in Vietnam as a naval officer out of Columbia University. Admiral Elmo Zumwalt selected him to be his aide when Zumwalt was the Navy's Chief of Naval Operations. He took David with him to the Pentagon.

A couple of years later, in 1970, Zumwalt was on the special train back to Washington D.C. after the Army-Navy football game with Henry Kissinger, who was a national security adviser. Kissinger was saying that he couldn't get good help anymore. On the spot, Zumwalt offered David Halperin to Henry Kissinger. So Halperin went over to work for Henry Kissinger in the West Wing of the White House, and the military aide to Kissinger at the time was Colonel Alexander Haig.

The idea of working at the White House was beyond my comprehension, even if I had written in my notebook that I could one day become a resident of the venue when I was at Hamilton. So, I didn't quite know what to say to David's suggestion. But I never brought it up again. Neither did David as I didn't see him for quite a while because he was a better squash player and moved on up the ladder—though we have since become the best of friends, and he's godfather to my son.

David went on to do some great things as a lawyer, working abroad in Hong Kong. He also had a very successful business career on top of his law practice. So, he came up big, too.

Back then, however, I was once again at loose ends. I had been turned down by the Harvard Business School because I did miserably on the Harvard Business School test, which was called the Admission Test for Graduate Study in Business. The head of the admissions committee at Harvard, who brought me into the Harvard admissions world and later became the president of the University of Utah, even wrote a letter of recommendation for me, and I still got turned down. Déjà vu.

We were coming into June 1973, and I was walking through Harvard Yard when this guy in a suit came up to me and asked, "Are you Chuck Wardell?" I said, "Yes." He then said, "Are you Charles W.B. Wardell the Third?" Again, I said yes. He then told me that he was from the Boston office of the FBI and that the White House was trying to reach me. He said I was to call operator 106 at the White House. Then he added, "Don't call collect because they don't accept collect calls."

So, I called operator 106 at the White House, and they put me through to Miss Gwin in General Haig's office. Miss Gwin, an intelligent and kind individual with a sharp wit, who would become a close friend, stated, "The plane is returning General Secretary Brezhnev to Washington from El Toro." I understood that she was referring to Leonid Brezhnev, the leader of the Soviet Union, who was traveling back on the president's plane. She then inquired, "Could you board the plane to return to El Toro as General Haig would like to conduct an interview with you at the Western White House? If you can get to Washington National Airport, I will have a White House car waiting to take you to Andrews Air Force Base so that you can fly out to California to meet General Haig." And I said, "I'd love to."

Sometimes people come through for you. Norman Thomas wrote the letter for me to attend Lake Forest College in Illinois, and now David Halperin had done the same. I saw, once again, what goodness looked like. David Halperin had done what he said he would do. It's a quality I greatly admire and have done my best to follow. For the rest of my life, I have done what I have said I'll do, and everybody knows it. That's where this quality in me came from. On a rainy day in March, Halperin told a guy whom he hardly knew, "You know, General Haig could use some help, and I think that would be a good first stepping stone for you." Then he did what he said he was going to do. He contacted General Haig, and now I had a job interview with him.

In fact, I even have a copy of the letter David sent. What he said about me still makes me proud. He wrote:

> *I am writing in part, General, to recommend a good friend of mine, Chuck Wardell—who would very much like to work for you and whom I regard as one of the finest people I know. He is graduating from Harvard this month with high academic honors and served in the Special Forces for years before coming to Harvard. He has the kind of absolute ability to get things done...*

I made it to National Airport, and they drove me to Andrews, and I walked onto Air Force One, but it wasn't a 747 back then. It was a customized version of Boeing's 707. The aircraft's tail number was 27000 so its call sign was SAM 27000 when the president wasn't on board.

You walked up the stairs on the airplane and, if you went straight on, you'd walk into the president's suite. If you turned left, you would be with the pilots. And if you turned to the right, there were four plush seats that were reserved for the first lady. Behind them was seating for staff, and behind them was seating for the media. As the president was already in California, I was ushered into the first lady's section. We took off, and I said to myself, "I can't quite believe that I'm sitting on Air Force One, in theory, flying to California to meet General Haig."

I will report more on what happened when I went to California in the next chapter, but I came back to Harvard, and the guy that Hamilton kicked out for being, in their estimation, an idiot, graduated *cum laude*.

And now, with my Harvard degree, I was going to enter the White House in 1973, the year that everything came apart for the Nixon administration because of Watergate. Once again, I was right in the middle of it all.

Chapter 6
"Access without authority."

Three years after being under pretty constant threat of violent death courtesy of the North Vietnamese, I was graduating from Harvard and now getting dressed in a hotel room in San Clemente, California to meet General Alexander Haig, chief of staff to President Richard Nixon. I put on my best suit, and I spritzed my shoes with hairspray, which is an old OCS trick to make them shine so brightly that you can see your reflection in them. Or at least think you can.

Muriel Hartley, General Haig's secretary, had sent me a note informing me that, at 8:50 on the morning of June 28, 1973, a car would pick me up from the San Clemente Inn, and they would try to get me in to see the general "at about 9 AM."

The Marine picked me up at the appointed time and drove me over to the Western White House, which was located in the Coast Guard station in San Clemente. I was sitting on the terrace overlooking the Pacific Ocean waiting to see General Haig along with some other people, including the actor Liv Ullman, the astronaut Neil Armstrong, Brent Scowcroft, who was the deputy assistant to the president for National Security Affairs, and Daniel Moynihan who was then the U.S. Ambassador to India and who had previously been my economics tutor at Harvard. Small world.

Nobody was giving speeches on the terrace as we waited. Once again, it was like Harvard in the sense that we were all there for a reason, and that was good enough.

So, nobody questioned why this kid was sitting there in his best suit and shiny shoes because people assumed I had done something right because I was here with them, and they knew why they were there, so it all connected.

Neil Armstrong had quite a bit to say while we were sitting there, and he told us the hardest things that he had ever done were to land an airplane on an aircraft carrier during the Korean War and to be in tip-top shape as an astronaut. He said that, during the Mercury program, NASA thought that in order to survive in space, you had to be at the highest level of fitness, which turned out not to be true. Neil Armstrong then looked at each one of us and said, "You know, you have a finite number of heartbeats. And I'm never going to waste one more of them by exercising."

I did not see General Haig at 9:00 AM. When lunchtime rolled around, I had a sandwich in the White House mess, which I did not have to pay for this time. Finally, around 3 o'clock in the afternoon, I got my meeting with the general.

We had more in common than I realized as Haig had not been a great student and could not get into West Point until he had spent two years at Notre Dame bumping up his grades. He graduated in the bottom third of his class, and he had served in the Korean War, commanding a battalion as well as a brigade in Vietnam. He had become Nixon's chief of staff after H.R. Haldeman resigned due to his role in Watergate. Haig was also the youngest four-star general in American history when we met, not yet fifty years old.

We sat on two chairs on a cement slab outside his

office overlooking the Pacific Ocean. I knew I was dealing with a four-star general, a brave man who had served his country and who had been awarded the Distinguished Service Cross, the Silver Star with oak leaf cluster, and the Purple Heart. I did not know what I was dealing with in terms of Watergate.

Watergate was a political scandal involving President Nixon's administration. It began on June 17, 1972, when a group connected to the president broke into the Democratic National Committee headquarters at the Watergate office building in Washington. The subsequent attempts to cover it up by the administration had put a lot of heat on the president and his office. Haig told me, "I'm the chief of staff, and I'm not going to get involved in it," meaning Watergate. I didn't know what the chief of staff did for the president. I didn't know anything about how it worked at all. Once again, I was in the psych class but I didn't know anything at all about psychology.

General Haig told me something quite interesting about how he saw his role as the president's chief of staff. He said that this was not a job where you serve one man, the president. His job was one where you kept your own counsel. And it was also a job where there was a great deal of tension. "But, if I bring you in, Chuck, it will be to do staff work."

I did not know what that was—yet. During that interview, I could never tell whether he had ever looked at my Vietnam record because all he had to do was call the Pentagon, and there I would be. He knew three things about me, though. He knew that I had graduated from the

Special Warfare School and that I had been a trigger puller in Vietnam. He knew I'd been decorated. And he knew that I was a graduate-to-be from Harvard College. He asked if I could pass an FBI Full Field investigation, and I said, "Yes, I could."

He said, "David Halperin is the reason you're here. I like him a lot. So why are you interested?"

I said, "Well, I'm not sure." That was not a great beginning, so I quickly continued, "I understand the concept of service. I think that I've earned my spurs in serving my country. I'd be flattered to be able to work for you, or the president, at any level or in any capacity."

We spoke for about twenty minutes, and I figured that he must have liked me well enough because there were a hell of a lot of other people who wanted to get inside the White House. Then he asked, "So what do you think of Watergate?"

Was there a right answer to this question?

"I don't know, General," I said. "But I think you guys are in for a fight."

He looked at me for a moment and said, "Chuck, if I bring you on board, I'm not doing you any favors."

I later learned that Professor Moynihan, who had been in to see General Haig before I did, noted to Haig that I would be meeting him, and that Moynihan knew me. He told the general, "I know you're going to see Chuck Wardell. He's out there waiting for you. You are not going to have any problems with his gray matter."

The fact that Moynihan said that still makes me feel proud today.

When I was leaving General Haig's office at San

Come Up Big

Clemente, Muriel Hartley, General Haig's secretary, said, "The president's coming." I stood there in anticipation of meeting my second president, though this time I was not waving at him from the side of the road; I was in the room.

President Nixon then walked in. I was surprised as the president was much taller than I had imagined that he would be, at just over six feet tall. Muriel Hartley kindly introduced me and pointed out that I might be working with General Haig. So, Richard Nixon stuck his hand out, and I stuck my hand out to shake hands. But then Nixon pulled his hand back, and so I pulled mine back, and we didn't shake. It was one of the most awkward moments of my life and, to this very day, it makes me blush.

Then the Marine Corps drove me to LAX, and I got on a commercial flight back to Boston, not on Air Force One this time as there was no foreign potentate to ferry back to D.C., and Nixon was staying in California for a while. On the flight back, I was thinking, "I'm never going to get hired at the White House. And that's fine. Because this was the experience of a lifetime."

I mean, the kid wrote in his Hamilton notebook that his address was the White House had just had a job interview for a position there. That was good enough. I would never have believed it even possible when I made that notation.

On my flight back to Boston, I was also thinking that two things had come together in my life. One, that my military career actually was worth something. I had learned about myself and I had learned how to be a leader in a very specific military context. I also knew there were things that applied beyond it. My Harvard professor Daniel Moynihan had told General Haig that Chuck Wardell was not stupid. Those two things stayed with me for the rest of my life.

I got back to Boston, and heard nothing from the White House. Or, at least, not directly. I did receive a full background check from the FBI because if the government hired me, I was going to be as close as you could be to the president. They wanted to make sure I wasn't going to cause trouble. They started with my life in kindergarten and worked their way up, talking to hundreds of people about me, looking for trends that could be red flags. So, I knew that I was at least under consideration.

After thirty days of hearing nothing from the White House, I wrote a letter to the chief of staff's office, telling the general, "I very much enjoyed meeting you, but I have other opportunities, and I need to get my career going." In truth, the White House was my only job opportunity, so I was being a touch nervy. I wanted to move the needle on my future, and this was the only way that I saw how. It worked.

Two days later, I got a call from the White House. They told me to report to work on August 6, 1973. I took that as being hired. I had never been to the White House and so, on August 6, I had to use a map to find out where it was. I walked down the long driveway at the northwest gate, past the Marine guards, and went into the receptionist's office and reported for duty. The very attractive Shelly Buchanan, the wife to Patrick

Buchanan, who was a longtime assistant to the president, was behind the big desk. I said, "I'm reporting for duty to work for General Haig."

She directed me down the hall and then to turn left, so I did as I was told and walked down that hall and into the chief of staff's office, arriving just one minute after 7 AM. I said, "Good morning." The general looked up at me with his stern countenance and said, "You're late." That is how I began my year and a bit of working in the West Wing of the White House.

I was told to go downstairs and talk to David Hoopes, the special assistant to the president. Hoopes was in his early thirties, so a bit older than me, and it might have been him in the rear of the jet with his family when I flew out to San Clemente. I figured this was not the time to inquire.

When he was just out of high school, David Hoopes had served his mission for the Church of Jesus Christ of Latter-day Saints in Argentina. When he returned, he went on to get his BA in political science and a master's degree in international public administration from Brigham Young University and next snagged a master's degree in public administration from the University of Southern California. He was, as they say, no slouch.

Hoopes said, "You're working for me." I said "I guess I am." And he said, "Here's something I want for you to write up." So, on my first morning, I, who struggle with dyslexia, had to write a paper on something Hoopes asked me to do. I thought to myself, "Okay, you can write this, you can do this. Just get your mind through it."

And, little by little, I began to get my groove down there in the basement of the White House, right next to the White House mess room, and across from what was in those days the barber shop. Three days into my job, I got a haircut from the barber, Milt Pitts. We talked about The Beatles. About three or four months later, in November or December, I moved upstairs to the little office that was off of General Haig's main office. Just down the hall from the Oval Office. What I had begun to realize now, in my time at the White House so far, was that there was a cult around any sitting president. There was jockeying for position to be around the president and to get close. I was close enough. I had status as I was in the West Wing, two doors down from the president of the United States. I parked my car in West Exec, the parking area between the White House and the Executive Office buildings. That's where the cool guys parked. I was a member of the White House Mess but I still didn't have a free lunch because I got a bill at the end of the month from the White House Mess. Nevertheless, I had all the credentials I needed, and I was also handling stuff that the president saw.

I have a funny story connected to the White House, via Teddy White, who I had hung out with at Harvard and watched drink a lot and he'd get my hackles up with his, shall we say, unschooled take on Vietnam. However, Teddy was a great journalist who wrote many books, along with the series *The Making of the President*, which included books he did on Nixon in 1968 and also 1972. He would even write one about Nixon's fall and

Watergate and even interviewed me for that book. He also wrote a nice note to me in one of his books.

White was working as a correspondent in China in the 1940s when Mao was ruthlessly building his empire. He met Zhou Enlai on the Great March, and they became friends. When Teddy left China to return to the United States, Zhou gave him a banquet. Teddy was seated beside Zhou, the revolutionary and statesman who was also the very first premier and foreign minister of the People's Republic of China from 1949 until his death in 1976. Dinner was a roasted pig. Teddy was Jewish, and said to Zhou, "I can't eat this. It's pork." Zhou looked Teddy White in the eye and said, "Nothing to worry about. It's a duck."

When Nixon went to China in 1972, White went along as well as part of the press corps. They were each assigned squares to stand on in the Forbidden City to be present for the president's appearance and, when the president and Zhou Enlai walked past Teddy, Zhou stopped right in front of Teddy who was short and wore glasses, and Zhou stared at him, and Teddy stared back. And then Zhou, who was brilliant, charming, and had a memory like a steel trap, said, "It's still a duck."

Teddy White was also the journalist that Jackie Kennedy called to come up to Hyannis Port a week after John F. Kennedy was killed to help her revise his legacy. He didn't know it at the time, as he was just trying to help a distraught young widow, but it was Teddy who wrote the piece in *Life* magazine that declared JFK's presidency to be like the court of King Arthur in Camelot, a time of elegance, bravery, and beauty, pretty much taking dictation from Jackie. White later described his comparison of JFK to Camelot as the result of kindness to the distraught widow of a just assassinated leader and wrote that his essay was a "misreading of history. The magic Camelot of John F. Kennedy never existed."

I pretty quickly learned that, if I had any notion that I was in or hoped to be in Camelot, I should think again. I started working in the White House in August 1973 and, by October, Richard Nixon needed a new vice president. Spiro Agnew had become the second vice president to resign after John C. Calhoun resigned in 1832 over political differences with President Andrew Jackson. Spiro Agnew had been the governor of Maryland for two years before Nixon tapped him to be his VP, and two years later he resigned over legal differences with the Department of Justice.

Agnew's troubles began in the summer of 1973 when he was investigated for extortion, bribery, and income-tax violations relating to his time as the Maryland executive in the 1960s when he was accused of taking bribes from construction companies, a practice that continued when he was governor of Maryland. Agnew fought the federal indictments, arguing that a sitting vice president could not be indicted. The only way he could be forced to go was by impeachment. When the solicitor general announced that vice presidents could be indicted, Agnew dug in and vowed not to resign.

However, the other problem was that his boss Richard Nixon was facing impeachment for his role in the Watergate scandal, and the Nixon administration didn't need the Agnew headache to complicate matters. Agnew's lawyers made a deal with a federal judge, and Agnew resigned from the vice presidency on October 10, 1973.

He appeared in the United States District Court in Baltimore to plead no contest to one federal count of failing to report on his income tax return in 1967 when he was governor of Maryland. Acknowledging that this plea would amount to having a felony conviction, Agnew declared that he would resign in the national interest. He was fined $10,000 and sentenced to three years of unsupervised probation.

What Spiro Agnew had really done was to trade government access for cash. It was the way things were done in Baltimore but, now that he was gone, I got to do a lot of the things nobody else wanted to do—like help him move out of his office. It didn't help that the movers who were supposed to show up at 6:30 PM arrived an hour early when Agnew was still in his office. So, what fell on me and a few others was to set up another office for him in the new Executive Office building, a couple blocks down from the old one. Then, I had the momentous task of getting parking passes so Agnew could drive himself to the office in the new Executive Office building. He was no longer subject to security after he resigned and had to sign himself in, as it were, so I went over and handed him his parking passes. Spiro Agnew was actually a delightful guy. He was very smart and had a great sense of humor. He didn't see anything wrong with the time-honored tradition of taking a few bucks in exchange for his political help. He hated Nixon, though, for not supporting him, and I believe that he lived the rest of his life without ever speaking to Nixon again, two or three times refusing to take the former president's call.

One of the things about working in the White House is that most staffers rarely see the president. The cabinet might see him once every four months. The staff sees him by appointment, with the exception of the most senior people, such as the Chief of Staff. You can't just go into the Oval Office and say, "Hi, boss." Most of the time I would put the president's papers on an empty desk in an empty office, which is how I came to sit in his chair at his desk in the Oval Office one snowy winter day when the White House was emptied due to weather, a photo of which is on the cover of this book. The other thing I did, rather, that I never did, was to tell Nixon that I had attended Harvard. Nixon hated Harvard men.

I did, though, speak to him from time to time. I would pass by him in the hall, and we'd stop and talk a little. He once said to me, "There are lessons in this town, Chuck, and one of them is don't want it so bad." It took me a long time to figure out what he meant, but I know now that he meant that naked ambition in D.C. was a dangerous thing and that you should always have a backup plan in case what you thought you wanted was not indeed what you really wanted. Or that Washington no longer wanted you.

He also said to me, "Chuck, they throw big rocks in this town, and you have to learn to pick them up and throw them back." I had a pretty good idea of what that meant. After Vietnam, I could deal with throwing rocks.

Come Up Big

In the White House, I did see evidence of what the Founders had wanted to achieve, the separation of powers, was real. The president has absolute power as commander-in-chief, but, on a day-to-day basis, what does he do? Does he walk into his room where sirens go off with people running here and there and putting state papers in his hands? No, in short.

There is an incredibly detailed process for how things get done. Paperwork makes its way up from Congress via a staff secretary. From there it travels around government staff for input. Eventually, it goes to the president's chief of staff. Then that paperwork goes to the president. There have already been a lot of eyeballs on the documents and input about them. It's not about presidential whim. And should never be.

Then there's the president's personal schedule. These appointments to see him are made months, even years, ahead of time. So, the president is reacting to a flow of information around him, much of which has been scheduled well in advance. One time, they had some Wisconsin Congressman, along with the fetching Miss Wisconsin and a noble cow, out waiting to meet President Nixon on the South Lawn of the White House. Nixon wondered "Why in the hell would I want to see them?" Well, came the reply, "You promised the Congressman in that district that you would meet with them, so here they are." There were a lot of meetings like that one. "Meet and greet" takes up an inordinate amount of time for the president.

If any member of the government wants to see the president, they cannot just walk into his office. For example, David Parker, who scheduled the president when I was in the White House, really controlled who the president saw. Also, few could call the president directly and, if they did, they would normally go through Rose Mary Woods, his senior assistant. She met Nixon while she was a secretary to the House Select Committee on Foreign Aid. She had been impressed by his neatness and accepted a job with him in 1951 and she hung on to the end. She was loyal and would even claim responsibility to a grand jury in 1974 that it was she who inadvertently erased up to five minutes of the missing eighteen-and-a-half minutes on the Watergate tapes.

The reality of our government is that the House controls the purse. The Senate controls the treaties. In the old days, the House would pay for war, the Senate would declare war, and the nation would fight it. The War Powers Act really changed all of that. It gives the president ninety days to commit troops to whatever war they think we need to fight.

When you consider it in terms of leadership, the White House does not fit the traditional model. We usually consider a leader to be in charge of everything or to be responsible for everything within their leadership realm. That's not the case in the White House because of the separation of powers and because the president is also the political head of their party. So, it's an unusual form of leadership compared to being, say, the CEO of the international executive search firm WittKieffer, which I would become, and where the board is whom I had to talk to and convince that my decisions were the right ones.

Come Up Big

To put it in perspective, imagine you're running Amazon. Now, once every four years, the people who work there vote on whether you get to come back and continue to run the company. The board gets to tell you whether or not you're not going to do this or that or whether you're going to Italy on your yacht or not. As the head of Amazon, you only have power on a day-to-day basis to put out a new product but, even then, you have a lot of constraints.

A sitting president is judged by whether or not their decisions will keep them in the job, decisions of both politics and policy. The other thing is that if the president doesn't control the House and the Senate, which mostly they do not, then he or she has even more constraints upon their power. The president's own policy initiatives then become suggestions. You can posture all you want but, in the end, the president is really the leader of the Constitution of the United States, which is based on the separation of powers.

The thing that I learned most about leadership in the White House is that the terms "leader" and "leadership" can hide many sins. And a successful leader, which could be whatever definition the people around the leader wanted to give, allowed the leader to hide the sins committed by the intrepid leader or even their government. And if you were not a successful leader, your sins would come out, which really means you were never a successful leader to begin with. So much of leadership is about not revealing what is actually behind the curtain.

Because of the Watergate investigation, and the

sins committed in the White House that were becoming public, there was an increasing tension in the White House. You could read about it in the newspapers and ironically, for me, the people I was reading about, the Mitchells and the Haldemans, were people I'd never met, but I certainly felt their legacy. I came into the White House after they had left. But, as Watergate began to break, the tension that it created led to an increasing sense of isolation within the White House because nobody was sure who knew what or who was going to get subpoenaed next.

Along with this isolation, there was a rising sense of general outrage. In 1973, the world was in a mess with the military coup in Chile led by General Augusto Pinochet, and the oil embargo declared by OPEC, which led to a global oil crisis, along with the Yom Kippur War between Israel and some Arab states, led by Egypt and Syria.

As for the war in Vietnam, in early January 1973, the U.S. and North Vietnamese had ironed out the last details of the settlement and both sides, including South Vietnam, signed the final agreement in Paris on January 27. As it would come to pass, only the United States honored the cease-fire as North Vietnam still wanted to conquer the South, and the South was united to stop them. So, they fought on.

Within twenty-four hours of the cease-fire, almost six hundred American prisoners of war began to come home along with the remaining American troops in South Vietnam, though the Marines stayed behind to look after institutions for a couple more years. In 1975, thirty North Vietnamese divisions finally succeeded in defeating the South. The American commitment to defend South Vietnam, described as airtight by both President Nixon and Secretary of State Kissinger, had been ambushed by the Watergate scandal. All the air had been expelled.

I was increasingly marginalized because I wasn't involved in anything that was going on around me as far as Watergate was concerned—though I did get called in to man the battle stations on Saturday night, October 20, 1973.

"So, in October of 1973, Chuck said, 'why don't you guys all come down, and I'll give you a tour of the White House?'" my Harvard friend Jack McLean recalled. "We thought that sounded like a pretty good idea. My wife and I and two of our friends hopped on a train one Friday night, and we went down, checked into a hotel, and then went out to Chuck's house in McLean, Virginia. And his red phone rang, and apparently it was the White House calling Chuck. He had to leave. About an hour later, Chuck re-emerged and said, 'They just went and fired Cox and Richardson.' It was the Saturday Night Massacre."

The Saturday Night Massacre, as it became known, happened when President Nixon ordered the firing of Archibald Cox, a Harvard law professor who was the special prosecutor investigating Watergate. The attorney general and his deputy refused to fire him and resigned, so the solicitor general reluctantly did it and, of course, the fallout was huge. But I didn't know it on that night. I just knew things were falling apart, and I had friends visiting me. "The next day was a beautiful fall day, and Chuck said, 'Come on over to the White House,'" Jack McLean recalled. "So, we went over. Nixon had left for Camp David and it was Sunday, so there was nobody there. Chuck gave us the full tour of the White House. It was pretty cool."

However, things at work were far from cool. Nixon was in deep trouble. When news of Nixon's taped conversations broke, and the fact that one tape was missing eighteen minutes of presidential talk, I was called down by the FBI to the old post office at 1100 Pennsylvania Avenue, a famous landmark that functioned then as a federal office building and which now belongs to the Waldorf Astoria Hotels chain. The FBI put me in a small room under a hot light blazing down, and two very serious FBI agents questioned me about the eighteen-and-a-half-minute gap in the tape. Did I handle it? Did I erase it? Did I know who did it? And my answer was, "No." But I knew that this was a warning shot across my bow to be incredibly careful.

Then the FBI appeared in the White House, trying to secure the offices as if the whole place was a crime scene. Nixon became increasingly isolated. General Haig became tougher to deal with. He was never mean to me, but now he ignored me. So, it was a little like going to work every day and being the guy who is sitting in a little office right outside the boss's front door and being ignored by the boss. It wasn't that he didn't trust me. He just kept me out of it for my own good.

In Vietnam, I was in a position to die. I wasn't going to get killed in the West Wing of the White House.

Come Up Big

But my career certainly could have died there. I could have easily been set up by somebody who didn't like me. I remember talking about the White House transcripts with Fred Buzhardt who was the general counsel at the Pentagon prior to being Nixon's lawyer for Watergate. In one of our conversations, he said to me about Nixon, "I like the guy. I'm just not gonna go to jail for him." So, there was a growing tension of "Holy shit. We could all wind up in jail."

About this time, I was also quoted in a *Newsweek* article on Watergate saying, "The shit's about to hit the fan."

As it was hitting the fan, I did have the support of Admiral Elmo Zumwalt. He was the chief of naval operations, the most senior admiral in the U.S. Navy, and the guy for whom my friend David Halperin had worked. Zumwalt was greatly disliked by the White House as well as by General Haig. I used to joke that I was the only person in Washington who had used both Admiral Zumwalt and General Haig as references. That was the only time the two of them would be in the same room, so to speak.

They disliked Zumwalt because of his efforts to reform the U.S. Navy, and his reform efforts were many. He wanted to bring in diversity and raise women to higher, more powerful posts. His Project 60 aimed to reduce the number of excess ships afloat within sixty days. He persuaded Congress to fund the F-14 jet, which had fewer manning and maintenance needs and would save money. The F-14s were part of the Navy from 1974 through 2006. He created a guided missile frigate featuring both increased capabilities and reduced cost. When he took over as chief of naval operations in 1970, the U.S. had aging ballistic missile submarines, which alarmed Zumwalt given the dangerous climate of the Cold War. He changed that, as well, and created the Ohio class ballistic missile sub, one of the best nuclear subs, which is still in service today.

He also wanted to "modernize and humanize" the Navy, and his communications to the Navy became known as "Z-grams." These included orders authorizing facial hair and longer hair for male sailors and, with the relaxed grooming order, he introduced beer-dispensing machines to naval barracks. He also expanded opportunities for female sailors, allowing for the assignment of women to ships, opening restricted Navy communities to women, and helping women to progress to "flag rank" (rear admiral and higher) after Senate approval. The first woman so promoted to admiral, Zumwalt kissed on the cheek. When he was asked about kissing a new admiral, he said, "I have kissed a lot of admirals, but this is the first one I have kissed on the cheek." He also worked to eliminate the racism that he saw and wanted to stop. So, what's not to like about the guy?

I loved him. He taught me a lot about what it means to be a true leader in a place where those qualities are not always appreciated because of rivalry and jealousy. He's the best leader that I've ever met. He was tough, but he had a very fine sense of humor; he was loyal to the people he commanded; and he was unassuming. Not a guy to swagger into the room. He won the Bronze Star

Come Up Big

for Valor in World War II in combat against the Japanese navy, and he graduated from the Naval Academy and rose to command the U.S. Navy in Vietnam. Then, at age 49 in 1970, the president appointed him to command the entire Navy as the youngest four-star admiral in its history.

I've tried to emulate his calm and confident style, and it took me years to achieve that state. His sense of self was enough to convey his authority when he told you something. He didn't have to tell you one more time. He was the real deal. He cared about people, they cared about him, and he loved the Navy.

I went to see him one time at the "Admiral's House," which is where, traditionally, the chief of naval operations lived. He was the last admiral to live in that house, which then became the residence for the vice president of the United States and remains so to this day. We sat on his balcony overlooking Washington Circle, drinking coffee. I got an idea of how he asserted his authority with a light touch during our conversation. I felt it and heard it when I made a comment about his Navy fliers, which he did not like. I said, "They went home to three hots and a cot [three hot meals a day and a bed], but I stayed, and I dug in." He could have gone berserk at this insult to the cushiness of the Navy compared to trying to dig into the jungles of Vietnam but, instead, I got the admiral's stare, and he said, "I don't understand your point, young man." I said, "I'm sure it was a poor one" and quickly changed the subject.

After he retired, he told me to call him Bud, which was his nickname, but I refused. I said, "No, you're the former chief of the country's naval operations, and I will call you Admiral." So, I did. When I was at the White House, we spoke about life and Washington and things that were happening. I got to know him and, eventually, we would smoke cigars in his sauna, which, shall we say, is an art form all its own.

I learned a lot about self-deprecation from Zumwalt. I learned that how you see yourself is how people will see you, too. That, combined with your ability to accomplish and do things. You don't have to tell people that you're a giant if you're a giant. They will either figure it out or not but telling them that just makes you look like a jackass. There were more than a few jackasses around in the White House, and it was a tense time as we moved into the spring and summer of 1974 with Watergate now becoming a major crisis.

As General Haig put it to me, I had "access without authority," which meant that I was in the room and heard things, but I kept my mouth shut. I was doing my best and, while I was working for very senior people, I wasn't a senior person, though I handled many of the president's briefing papers. I was a witness to history as the debris of Watergate rained down upon us.

It was May 1974, and I got involved in Watergate in two ways. The U.S. Supreme Court had ruled that President Nixon had to release the Oval Office tapes to government investigators of the Watergate burglary. So, I had to get the tapes transcribed. There was a picture on the front page of the *New York Daily News* of a guy lugging the transcriptions up to the House to deliver them to the impeachment committee. That guy was me.

Come Up Big

One Sunday afternoon, I got a call from Camp David from General George Joulwan, General Haig's close friend and assistant, telling me that there was a particular tape that they needed to hear and asked if I would arrange to have it driven up to Camp David. He also wanted to know if the president had listened to it, and I said I would check, but I didn't know. Then I arranged to have it transported to Camp David, which is about sixty-five miles northwest of Washington, D.C. in the Maryland mountains. That was the "smoking gun" tape which revealed that the president had indeed conspired to cover up activities that took place after the burglary and then tried to obstruct the investigation, and this tape was one of the earliest ones in which the cover up began. They all listened to that smoking gun tape at Camp David and concluded that saving this administration was hopeless. We all knew this.

So, I was working with a lot of angry people in that summer of 1974. It was the second time in my life that I had found myself on the wrong side of history. I lost half my friends when I went to Vietnam and the other half when I went to work for the Nixon administration. I didn't have a group to hang out with and have a beer on Fridays after work. It was not like that around the Nixon White House. I was on my own once again—but then, so were we all.

It was one of my duties to put the president's briefing papers on his desk at night, and I continued to do so. At the end, when Senator Barry Goldwater said he wanted to come talk to President Nixon with a few other senators, I ferried Nixon's briefing paper for that meeting, which I put at the front of the president's desk. Those papers were on the economy. When we were walking to that meeting from the Chief of Staff's office past the Roosevelt Room to the Cabinet Office, it was then that General Haig said to me, "No wall sitters." Which meant that no one would get a chair along the wall to watch the drama unfold.

So, it was the senators along with Nixon and General Haig in the meeting. Nixon started by saying, "I'd like to talk about the economy." And Goldwater said, "That's not why we're here." The jig, and the presidency, was up.

I was there when General Haig's assistant, Muriel Hartley, typed President's Nixon's letter of resignation. She slammed a piece of paper in an IBM 365 and typed, "I will resign the presidency as of August 8, 1974." I took it up to General Haig who was in the White House residence. I got off the elevator, and the usher and a Secret Service agent were waiting in the lobby outside the elevator, and they escorted me along a corridor that is like a long railroad car leading to the residence. I was going to the Lincoln Sitting Room, a parlor on the second floor of the White House that was once an office and telegraph room. It's located next to the Lincoln Bedroom and is furnished in a Victorian style to match the bedroom. Nixon loved it so much that he had it recreated in his presidential library.

It was here that I handed General Haig the letter, and he looked at this single piece of paper and said, "This isn't staff work." By that he meant that he wanted three or four choices for the president to have on his desk on which to sign his resignation.

There was a thirty-four-page competing version of Nixon's resignation announcement to contend with, written by Ray Price, the president's main speechwriter. People were shouting and angry and tired, and the West Wing was no joy. Much later, I understood from Pat Buchanan's book *Nixon's White House Wars: The Battles That Made and Broke a President and Divided America Forever* that the Ray Price resignation letter was left on the president's desk in the Oval Office. I do not know if it was ever signed, but President Nixon eventually signed the letter that I delivered, and he resigned.

Nixon came downstairs the next morning after he resigned, looking tired. I was in the state dining room, standing on the base of one of the golden light stands there and listening to him in a very subdued room. He talked for quite a while about his presidency, but one thing I remember is when he said, "Don't hate your enemies because that will destroy you." The blades on the waiting helicopter were whirring while the president was speaking and, in those days, the helicopter faced a great danger of overheating if he talked for too long.

It flashed through my mind just how ironic it would be if they had to shut down the helicopter just as Nixon was preparing to leave. But he finished speaking just in time and boarded the helicopter and left. Gerald Ford was now the president, and he got the nuclear codes when Nixon was over Jefferson City, Missouri. They are contained in a "nuclear football," that is a forty-five-pound aluminum-framed black leather briefcase, which is officially called the Presidential Emergency Satchel. It got its nickname as the "nuclear football" as it originated from Operation Dropkick, a nuclear attack plan codenamed "Dropkick."

There were four things in the briefcase when Ford got it. There was a book that explained the U.S.'s options to retaliate against anyone who fired nuclear missiles at us; a book listing classified nuclear missile site locations; a manila folder containing about ten pages that outlined what the Emergency Broadcast System needed to do in the event that nuclear missiles were fired at us; and a three-by-five inch card with the authentication codes to launch nuclear war on the world. The Russians were told when and where the transfer would be made in case they had any Cold War ideas to take advantage of Nixon's resignation.

The White House staff had considered that I might go west with Richard Nixon to be his aide in San Clemente, but then they reconsidered it. Haig thought I was too junior to do it as I was just twenty-nine years old at the time and had spent less than two years at the White House—even if they were two very long years spent during the Watergate investigation. This was actually good because I didn't want to do it. General Haig was eventually appointed vice Chief of Staff of the Army and, later, Supreme Allied Commander in Europe, arranged by Henry Kissinger with President Ford. I was left behind to welcome Dick Cheney and Donald Rumsfeld who were moving into my space as part of the Ford administration. I was moved upstairs in the West Wing.

Though he had spent only three years in the Navy, Rumsfeld went on to political stardom as both the youngest then the oldest secretary of defense under Ford from 1975 to 1977 and again from 2001 to 2006 under Bush. As for Cheney, who would go on to become George W. Bush's powerful vice president, he was only a White House intern before he was made chief of staff at age thirty-four—just five years older than me.

The night before Cheney and Rumsfeld moved in, I was making the chief of staff's office ready for them. There was a safe in the office and, since none of us had the code for it, the Secret Service drilled in. There was more than three hundred thousand dollars in cash inside the safe. Nobody knew what to do with this money, and nobody wanted to take it because everyone was so paranoid. So, I believe we gave the "found" money to the Air Force as payment for the political flights that President Nixon had taken on Air Force One.

The safe's contents made me curious about what was in my little office. I looked under my desk, and there was a box that I thought was just a footrest. I took the cover off and now realized that it was a tape recorder. I had never used it, but who knew what was on it? So, I called the White House phone representative, and they came in and took it out.

While I was doing all of this, I had to contend with the mice that we had running all over the place. The White House was full of mice because staffers ate at their desks all the time, so the mice would dart out as I was on the ground checking under desks. I would think, "If only the American public could see this glamor." When all was done, I left and arrived home about 4:30 AM. A few hours later, Cheney and Rumsfeld were installed, and I was out.

I told General Haig that I wanted to be a deputy assistant secretary of state for foreign assistance at the State Department, a job that examined how we spent our money abroad. As it was a presidential appointment, President Ford had to approve it. Haig was supposed to ask him to do it before Rumsfeld and Cheney moved in. Haig had still not asked, and I was heading back to that no man's land in which I wondered what I was going to do next.

General Haig eventually signed off and sent on the recommendations to Henry Kissinger, who sent it to Ford. Weeks passed, and then one Sunday afternoon I got called in to see President Ford. He signed my transfer to State with a very dubious expression. I understand that Ford later said to Haig about my transfer, "Well, it's on your head, Al."

Kissinger was even more dubious. He had been a soldier in the Battle of the Bulge, earning the Bronze Star. Then, after graduating from Harvard with a PhD in political science, he became Nixon's national security advisor in 1969, then secretary of state, and he remained so for Ford.

Kissinger decided that I would be a trial balloon. He told General Haig, "Send him there for six months as a special project officer. If the press doesn't pick it up, then keep him there and promote him." That was my entire interview for a presidential appointment, which I'd keep so long as I didn't end up on the front page of the

Washington Post. I'd already made the front of the *New York Daily News*.

I left the White House in December 1974 and as a going away gift, President Ford gave me a tube of Chapstick, framed. On the back of the frame was a rhyme about me, for me.

AN ODE TO CHUCK
or
HOW TO SUCCEED IN GOVERNMENT WITHOUT REALLY TRYING

Nixon, Ford, Haig or Rummy,
It mattered not, to this dummy,

Gopher Wardell would do their bidding,
And for great reward? Are you kidding!!!!

Yes sir, Yes sir!! He cried into the night,
I'll do it, I'll do it and hard as I might

Through tapes and transcripts and minefields he trod
We've never seen better luck, by God!!

Was it really just dumb Irish luck??
Hell no! That's why we call him "Chapstick Chuck"!!

I served as a special assistant doing this and that until May 1975. I was appointed to the Department of

State on May 7, 1975, and I got processed in, and my reception could not have been more hostile or chilly. To the bureaucracy within, meaning those career State Department officials, I represented everything that was wrong in the political world. I was there because the president had appointed me. They were asking, "Who is this kid, and what the hell is he doing here?"

As in the military before, where I was not a career soldier, here I was not a career foreign service officer but a political appointee. I also went to the State Department as an FS1—the highest rank of foreign service.

The saving grace was that I knew I would be leaving the State Department eventually. But it was a cold place while I was there. They were always looking for a reason to throw my ass out on to the street. I thought that they might even leak something to the press about how I got there as a political appointee. People are nasty. I was making $42,500 in 1974, which is equal to $282,180 today. I was at the top of the government at an incredibly young age. I had been a huge success, but I didn't know it. Everybody else did. And they hated me for it.

The work was grinding a lot of the time, and I didn't know diplomacy at all. Even so, I had the equivalent rank to a three-star general when I traveled on behalf of the State. I went over to South Korea to look at arms production and some security issues. It was a wild time in South Korea as we had discovered their nuclear weapons program that year. The embassy greeted me on my arrival, and the South Koreans lined up the troops to be inspected as they had been told of my three-star rank.

I was given gifts, and they flew airplanes above me and lined up Jeeps on the streets with troops saluting me. I was a big deal. I was a noticeably young man, just thirty years old, but I had to act the part of this three-star government potentate. I figured I would do my best.

The American ambassador's aide to South Korea and I were speaking on the phone one night, and the line went dead, which meant The Agency, theirs or ours, was listening. In fact, everybody thought I was CIA. I wasn't a CIA person. I was a State Department person who worked with the CIA when they needed my help, but I was in no way any kind of agent.

They sent me all across the world. I went to Kenya, and there are pictures of me with Madam Kenyatta, the wife of President Jomo Kenyatta. I went to Latin America and to Europe. I inspected the armament industry in Southern France. There was a factory clandestinely selling shells to Libya. And the gunpowder was coming from Sweden. Not good. Now we knew. Could we or would we do anything about it?

In England, I received a special tour of Churchill's wartime bunker. It was a very small room where the chiefs of the Army and the Navy and Churchill plotted strategy. It had vents because they all smoked in those days. I could see the gouges in the wooden arm of Churchill's chair because he had scraped his ring against the wood as a kind of nervous twitch. I wanted to sit in this chair and, as I was about to do so, I was grabbed by the head of security who said, "Nobody has sat in that chair since Churchill!" I did not sit in the chair.

I walked down the hall of the bunker and saw that

the WC was occupied, which seemed odd. However, it wasn't a washroom; it was a phone booth, where Churchill would speak to President Roosevelt about the state of the war.

Traveling the world with a black diplomatic passport, known as a "DIP," was excellent. I was a deputy assistant secretary of state appointed by the president and approved by the Secretary of State. I had auditors who worked for me to follow the money that had been sent abroad, to see if the countries that we had sent the money to were using it the way the U.S. government had intended. Which was never. Sometimes that was a problem.

What was often a problem was my State Department status, which not everyone believed. I got stopped by the authorities in Zaire, who thought I was CIA. They took my passport and held me in a small room in the airport for a couple of days. I told them, "You know, I'm here as a representative of the president of the United States." They said, "We don't care. Leave." I was made to feel most unwelcome. I would not be getting my job done investigating U.S. support of Zaire, so I left for home never having unpacked my bags. Sometimes members of my host country were even more blunt. I was having lunch in one of the new towers in Kuwait City. A Kuwaiti guy came up to me and said, "Are you Charles Wardell?" I said that I was, and he said, "Get up, go to the airport, and leave." And I said, "Okay" and did exactly what he asked. I never went back to the hotel, so I never picked up my clothes. I went right to the airport. It could have been a joke. It could have been a test. I figured I would work with the latter scenario in which I would likely live longer, so I left.

The long dark shadow of possibly being a CIA agent still follows me. A few years ago, I was attending a regional Economic Forum in China, prior to the big meeting in Davos, Switzerland. I was on the street outside of the Hyatt Hotel, and a very attractive young woman came up to me. She said, "I'm from Beijing International Studies University here, and I'm learning English. And you look like you speak English. I would love to learn how to speak English with you. Would you be a U.S. businessman?" I said, "I am." And she said, "Well, let's have coffee and talk English." I said, "I'd love to."

So, we went around the corner to a coffee shop, and we sat down. And I said, "Tell your masters that I'm here in China for a short time. I'm going to the Davos conference. I'm on a panel. This is where I'm going. I'm spending two nights there. I'm coming back here. I'm leaving the next day. That's exactly my schedule." And she said, "I just want to learn English." And I said, "Well, go practice your Chinese." I have not been back to China.

When I worked for the State Department, the staff had faith in my boss, Secretary of State Henry Kissinger. But he had been sucked into Watergate, and I did not associate with him. I went to the secretary of state's meetings once a month, but he was never there. He was always represented by a deputy but, even so, he knew I was there.

He died in 2023 at the age of one hundred years

but, while he was alive, I would see him from time to time. We both belonged to the Brook Club in Manhattan whose name comes from the Alfred Lord Tennyson poem "The Brook," whose line "For men may come and men may go, but I go on forever" is something that I had learned well in Washington—the coming and going part. When I would see Kissinger, I would always say, "Mr. Secretary, nice to see you." With Kissinger, you called him by the title he had when you worked with him. Upon my greeting, he always looked at me and said, "Jack, Jack, no resumes. I can't be helpful." He never got my name right. I stopped trying to correct that a long time ago and now, it doesn't matter.

In 2009, Kissinger was awarded the Thatcher Medal of Freedom in London. A small dinner of probably six or seven tables gathered to celebrate Henry Kissinger, hosted by Margaret Thatcher. She was out of office and beginning to fail. I was invited.

I loved it because, on the bottom of the invitation, it said, "Carriages at 10." They're very clear about what time they're kicking you out. At the dinner, I went up to Kissinger to congratulate him, and he gave me a look that said, "How the hell did you end up here?" It's a question I have asked myself many times in my life.

Kissinger, and also Cheney and Rumsfeld, enjoyed long political careers, but I could see the light at the end of my tunnel was going to shut off. Gerald Ford lost the 1976 presidential election to Jimmy Carter, and I knew my time was up. I got paged off a plane in Miami, and I was told that the White House wanted to speak to me. It was the head of human resources on the phone who told me that Jimmy Carter had accepted my resignation. I was now thirty-one years old, and I was jobless once again. So, I stood in the Miami airport and asked myself a question I had asked many times before: "What the hell am I going to do next?"

Chapter 7
"Steaming down the hallway with hot news."

I had left the Department of State and now had to find something else to do. Friends and mentors were good to me, and they stepped up yet again. I got an interview with the famous Maurice Raymond "Hank" Greenberg at the insurance giant AIG. Greenberg was a friend of Admiral Zumwalt's, and he had served in the Army, taking part in the invasion of Normandy and the liberation of the Dachau concentration camp. He also served in the Korean War as a captain, and he received the Bronze Star and the French Legion of Honor. He's still around and turned one hundred years old in May 2025.

Greenberg offered me a job at half my government salary along with the opportunity to go to AIG's Insurance University. If I did well enough at Insurance U, this would qualify me to work at AIG. The hair on the back of my neck rose up when he said this because I didn't think there was a chance in hell that I could survive Insurance University, let alone triumph. So, AIG was not for me.

Once again, a friend came to help me out, and this was my great friend from childhood, Dwight Miller. School had been good to Dwight and he to it, graduating at the top of the Hotchkiss School, then from Yale University, and then from the University of Virginia Law School. He was now a lawyer with Winthrop, Stimson, Putnam & Roberts, one of the biggest law firms in the

Come Up Big

U.S. and had been doing some legal work for American Express. Dwight told them that they should meet me, so Amex invited me in.

I was interviewed by George Waters, the father of the American Express card, and Jim Robinson, the new young CEO—or should I say James Dixon Robinson III who came from a big-money family in Atlanta and went to all the right schools, including Harvard for an MBA. He was CEO of Amex from 1977 until his retirement in 1993. Because of my work at the White House and at the State Department, I had credibility. I also told them what I did not have. I said, "I'm not analytical." They said that didn't matter as they were looking for general management in the firm. I had managed to survive Vietnam, the White House, and Watergate, and I figured that I was doing all right in the management area from staying alive to staying out of jail.

The interview went well. The plush offices of James Robinson and George Waters weren't unlike the plush offices of the West Wing of the White House and, when they offered me a job, I said, "Yes." I soon found out that I had, once again, snagged a job that was ahead of my skills.

I had no real sense of the difficulty of the dive I was making. For instance, I asked Jim Robinson what P&L meant (profit and loss), and I remember him saying, "It's going to be a very long year for both of us." I also, to this day, don't know why a balance sheet should balance. I understand that it's a long-term requirement in GAAP accounting, but the need for it has never struck me as overwhelmingly necessary.

I was starting at the top, and I knew that I had to find a way to be accepted, to learn what I needed to learn, and to find a niche in this big organization. As I went along, I began to realize that I had lost my sense of vertical fear, so I plunged in. I appreciated who my bosses were, but I began to realize that, in corporate life, the CEO is a God-like figure. He's almost like the Raj in the Punjab. He has his own Air Force. He has his own fleet of cars. He has anything he needs. And I began to see that big time corporate life presented one more set of skills that I needed to develop to survive in this corporate world—about half of which I think is political.

I also realized that, for most of the workers in it, this was their dash for glory. Between the ages of thirty-five and forty-eight, we see workers making this great dash; then, after age forty-nine arrives, ninety percent of workers think they somehow got screwed because they are not where they thought they should be. As George Waters used to say, "Is it fair? No. Is it the real world? Yes." What surprised me about corporate life, starting at the top, was the ferocity of the herd trying to get ahead. It made things cutthroat at times, but I'd seen the political infighting in the military, in the West Wing, and in the State Department. Hell, I'd fought in Vietnam. And I wasn't scared of the politics in corporate life.

My title was Special Assistant for Special Projects to the CEO, Jim Robinson, but I really worked for George Waters. He not only invented the American Express card, but he also invented credit cards. When Amex brought him on in 1961 as the general manager, Amex was still unprofitable, and management was unsure about the future. Waters' plan was to build up their "card," which was cardboard and purple, as was the Amex logo, and only worked at a couple of restaurants in New York City. George thought long and hard about what to do, and he essentially brought the plastic card to the U.S.

What George had pulled off was a Steve Jobs type of accomplishment. Imagine, in 1961, producing a colored piece of plastic in exchange for goods or services, one that guarantees the vendor will be paid. George not only did that, but he also managed to get hotels, airlines, restaurants, and businesses to buy in and sign up.

George Waters was a giant, but he was unappreciated at American Express because he wasn't part of the white shoe crowd. He was never made a director, which I thought was a travesty, but he was the father of the American Express card, which became the guiding light for all credit cards.

The reason the Amex card is green is because George Waters wanted it to look like money. He went to CEO Tom Watson at IBM and asked him for his help with card identification. IBM put a stripe on the back of the card, a stripe which IBM's Forrest Perry had invented for government procurement cards to help the government keep track of supplies in the supply chain. George put it on his credit card to help track billing. Of course, everybody else has since copied him. The stripe is still owned by the government, and IBM has never made any money from it.

I learned a lot from George, just by hanging around

him and asking questions. He always told me, "Lead the industry." He's the person who made people think a worthless piece of plastic was worth something and, if you change the color, it was even more prestigious. No matter what, be it a green card, a black card, a gold card, or a platinum card, they all run on the same railroad tracks. He used to tell me, "Don't sell the steak; sell the sizzle."

He was also the father of travel insurance. It's the most profitable product American Express has ever had. If you were making a short trip, you could buy a two-hour term life policy. It was genius.

People forget that when he took over American Express, he had to convince the airlines, hotels, and restaurants to say yes, they would accept this card. He also had to build the sales force to sell it. And he had to build the advertising to create the concept of using and accepting a worthless piece of plastic at a place that you might never go back to but where the vendor—and every vendor—was going to get paid. He figured out the economics of it all.

I saw that the strategy worked. On the strength of its advertising and growing list of participating businesses, the Amex Card had already turned a profit in one year under George and, by 1964, Amex sales surpassed those of Diners Club.

American Express, to this day, is the only credit card known to the big wide world as a T and E card—which means travel and entertainment—that pays all the bills created on that card. Visa and Mastercard bills are paid by merchant banks. If you have a card issued by

Visa, it is not Visa who is paying your debt. The merchant bank is paying.

When I joined American Express, George Waters was a gruff guy in his early sixties. He was dyslexic, but he didn't know it, and I didn't intend to point it out. Many people were scared of George, but I was not one of them. It wasn't that I was not impressed and grateful. I got to see the inside workings of "big time" corporate life. Like many jobs I have had, I was given a view from the top, as I had in the White House. I was lucky to have had access to the White House but had no authority. Now I was getting access and authority.

Still, getting all the access and authority that the job required took quite some time and some doing. Part of the inaccessibility was due to the fact people were skeptical of me, including Lou Gerstner, who was then president of American Express, and who I was told by a reliable source had said that "Wardell's just full of hot air." When I heard that, I thought he was probably right because I certainly wasn't analytical.

When I went to American Express, being a strategy puke was the way to get to the top. I remember being told that management was just for "mechanics," and that anybody at all could manage a company, but the person with the great mind who set out the strategy would win.

I believe the link between strategy and execution, or management, is people. My skills were with people. My skills were getting people, whom I didn't know, to do things that they didn't want to do—but that they needed to do for the common good. My people skills were battle-tested in Vietnam, in the White House, and also across half the world thanks to my tour of duty with the State Department. So, from the beginning, I didn't have the basic background or skills to be like a McKinsey-trained MBA steaming down the hall with the latest strategic nuance of some problem in Southeast Asia.

But I also didn't fear it.

For some reason, I wasn't worried about my career. I didn't see this as a great dash for glory, most likely because every job that I had worked in had ended. So, I saw no reason why, at some point down the road, I would not move on to something else. By definition, your time in college ends. By definition, your military assignment is up. When I left the White House, I got a Xeroxed piece of paper—back then they called photocopies "Xeroxes"—that said, among other things, "You're no longer authorized to use this facility." It was a pretty straightforward message to be gone.

So, as I started in the private sector, I saw it as a bridge to who knows what? I didn't see it as the place to make my final stand. Also, I never had the confidence to think of it as a place I would one day run as the boss. I was reminded of what they had long ago put in my Taft yearbook when my fellow students said that I "reminded them of a cliché."

This was not an inspiring endorsement from my contemporaries at the time, and it was one that I carried with me. It's a good example of the poisonous epithets people in high school say, which the person they said it about doesn't forget easily. But, I didn't come in with a "Look at me!" attitude at all. I came in trying to find my way in the private sector, to figure out how to survive, and to try to figure out what was going on around me, which was not unlike how to survive in the West Wing of the White House. It was certainly not unlike how to survive in an Army combat environment, minus the bombs and bullets. But survive I did.

Not only were people very suspicious of me because of my White House work, but also because of how I got hired. I was about two months into the job, and the head of personnel came up to me in the executive dining room and said, "Oh, you're Wardell. You're the only resume I ever got from the CEO that said, 'hire him.' Usually, I am the one making those decisions."

I went to a Jim Robinson staff meeting that he held every Thursday morning at 6:30 AM in his office. So, I had to get up at zero dark thirty to make it there on time. Jim had been appointed CEO at American Express about three months before my arrival, and I remember seeing one of his pay stubs lying on his desk. His base pay when he started at Amex in 1978 was $168,000 a year, which today would be $829,844.

I thought this was all the money in the world, and I am sure he had other compensation in the form of stock options and so on, but I remember this stub was just lying on his desk. He was also young for the job, having started at age forty-two, which people began to suspect, but I was still very young, too. I was in my early thirties, and I was incredibly young to be swimming at the corporate level I was at.

Despite my youth and the suspicions of me by some, things were going well at Amex because both

George Waters and Jim Robinson saw value in me. They wanted me to have bigger portfolios and trusted me to fly the Amex flag abroad. I was sent to Brighton, England to the Amex operating center. As soon as I arrived in the UK, I got malaria, and I ended up in a nursing home in Hove, England.

    I first met up with malaria while serving in Vietnam, but technically it was what they called a "fever of unknown origin" because malaria had been so bastardized by the French trying to cure it that the Americans had classified it as this generic thing—but, yes, it was malaria. I also got cholera and the black plague, which killed twenty-five percent of the population back in the fourteenth century, and here it was still with us. By the time I landed in the hospital in Hove, I had been given my immunization shots, and I'd taken my malaria pills, but malaria sticks around in your system. You get a remarkably high fever, your teeth chatter, and then eventually it goes away.

    I was still in the sweating and shaking portion of malaria in that Hove hospital, the morning after I was admitted, Margaret Thatcher had won the election to become the prime minister of the UK. On the TV in my hospital room was Janet McLuckie Brown, a female comic who impersonated politicians. I was still feverish and watching the TV, and I thought this comedian was really the new British prime minister. At first, I thought the woman was insane, which I know some people thought Thatcher really was, and then I realized it was all make believe. That was my first week working for Amex in England.

After surviving malaria in Brighton, I was then dispatched to London to run the international airline business for Amex. I lived in Belgravia, which is not too bad an address to have in the city, and I kept learning the ways of the green airline card.

I also had a whole new learning curve to navigate. I also had the feeling that I didn't know what I was doing at home or abroad, and so this acted as a kind of motivation to keep my mouth shut and watch what others were doing.

So I chose to do that very thing, and my corporate stock continued to rise. George Waters next sent me to Manama, Bahrain. He said to me "Go run the place." I said "Okay." So off I went to run Amex's operations in the Middle East.

Bahrain was a more liberal country than its neighbor, Saudi Arabia, and still separated by the waters of the Arabian Gulf. The fifteen-mile-long King Fahd causeway between the two countries had not yet been built, but Bahrain was still a culture shock to me after swinging London. I was busy running Amex from our little office by the Holiday Inn and trying to navigate this patriarchal Middle Eastern culture, but I lived in an expat community that was mainly made up of Brits, so I did still connect with some of that London style.

I was locked out of Bahrain by the heir apparent who today is the Emir of Bahrain. He tried to use his Amex gold card in San Francisco in an ATM to get money, and the American Express card just does not work at an ATM.

So, he threw me out of Bahrain, because he had

lost face. He thought I was thrown out forever, but I actually was thrown into the transit lounge at the airport, and ignored for forty-eight hours, and then told to go home. As in, back home to Bahrain, which is where I went.

I had another interesting experience while in Bahrain with another royal kid. Prince Bandar, the eldest son by his first wife of the then-sitting king of Saudi Arabia, had charged $6 million on his American Express card during some shopping splurge in Paris made by his retinue. I don't think it was money spent by Prince Bandar, not by any means. But it was on his card. Then he didn't pay us. Then he tried to pay the bill with a bad check, which is extremely poor form in the Middle East. Or anywhere, for that matter.

American Express had done everything they could to collect the money. It may still be the largest single card debt that they have ever had. They went and made the case to the Royal Diwan, which is the chief executive office of the king of Saudi Arabia. All kinds of corporate hands were wringing, but there was no result. The bill had not been paid.

In my "out of the box" thinking, a classic example of how I saw the world versus how Amex saw it with all of its lawyers pounding on the Diwan and getting no response, I went to my great friend, Admiral Zumwalt, who had retired from the Navy. He had a relationship with Saudi Arabia as he helped them to build up their Navy. I asked him if he could help me. Of course, he said, "Yes."

Admiral Zumwalt and I met with the ambassador

from Saudi Arabia in Washington on a pleasant March day. Rather, I remember sitting outside on the steps of the embassy building while the good admiral went in alone. He told the ambassador that Prince Bandar owed Amex $6 million and hadn't paid up. The ambassador told Admiral Zumwalt that he would make an inquiry.

Months later, I got a call from the Saudi embassy. I went down to see the ambassador. He said, "I've talked with the king, and we don't pay interest on debts."

I said, "I know. We just want what he owes us." Then he opened his checkbook, and he said, "Do I make this check out to you or to American Express?" I thought about it for a millisecond, and I said, "To American Express, please."

I went to the bank with his check, and they told me that the money was not in his official checking account. So, I had to call the embassy and have the $6 million transferred. It was, and the bill was paid. Had I resigned from American Express and collected it under the collection laws, I probably would be entitled to half the money, but I did not. In the end, for my efforts, I was given a $2,500 bonus for collecting $6 million.

Admiral Zumwalt wrote a letter to Amex's chairman Jim Robinson about it all, and this is what he said:

ADMIRAL ZUMWALT & ASSOCIATES, INC.
1500 Wilson Boulevard Arlington Virginia
22209 ELMO R. ZUMWALT, JR. President

12 September 1980 Mr. James Robinson

Charles W. B. Wardell III

Chairman of the Board
American Express Company, American Express Plaza, New York, New York 10004

Dear Jim,

Thank you for your letter of August 15. Now that our business matter has been successfully completed, I want to make a comment about Chuck Wardell.

Chuck's strategy for the conduct of this negotiation, particularly his concept that the solution could never be found at the other end and had to be initiated from Washington, and the flawlessness with which he dealt with the various nuances, were noteworthy. My own willingness to take on this assignment was the result of my firsthand knowledge of Chuck's character and integrity.

You have quite a remarkable person in this young man.

Sincerely,
E.R. Zumwalt, Jr.
cc. Chuck Wardell

It was a very fine gesture on the admiral's part to acknowledge me and my work to resolve this matter, and I was grateful. Despite having to run down deadbeat princes, I liked living overseas. It's a very delicate balance that you have to create because, unless you're going to be a career expat, which I was not, then you want to maintain focus on getting back to the parent company. You do that so that, when you finally land back home, you are real competition to the people who had never left.

While I was doing my thing in the Middle East, I was getting noticed beyond the walls of Amex, and so I was recruited to run a startup company called Highstoy. It was a private venture firm that made scanners of your carotid arteries. The concept of artery scanning was new in the 1980s, and people didn't really know what ultrasound was yet. The scanners were great, but the company struggled. When we had the opportunity to sell the company to a major pharmaceutical company, I was all in.

I entered the meeting with the major pharmaceutical company saying, "I think this company is worth $20 million." They said, "We think it's worth $500,000," and I said, "Sold!" One of the people on the Highstoy board of directors was Edward Teller, the father of the hydrogen bomb. He was a fascinating man to talk with, but he was a man of science, and we needed an infusion of cash to save the company.

Along the way, I learned a lot about small company struggles. One of my favorite stories and, as Henry Kissinger used to say, "It has the added advantage of being true," was when we couldn't pay our bills, and I needed to get some legal help. Syd Platzer was the bankruptcy attorney that I was recommended to hire.

When I first went to meet him, I climbed up the stairs to his office on Eighth Avenue in Manhattan and entered. He greeted me with the words, "I hate people like you. I don't work with people like you and, if I do, it's only for keyash." Well, I didn't understand that he meant "cash" when he said "keyash" in his Brooklyn accent, but I eventually caught on and paid him $5,000. We became very good friends. His firm still bears his name.

I had to meet the vendors to whom Highstoy owed money at the Holiday Inn on Long Island Expressway off exit 63. I was sitting at a table with Syd along with a few of my senior guys, and in front of me were the people we owed. One guy named Marcus kept screaming that I was stealing from them, had ruined their kids' lives, and should be in jail. He went on about what an awful person I was. I was nervous. I thought that I was the most conscientious CEO around. I had not been stealing. I had been trying to save the company. I told Syd we had thirty cents on the dollar to offer them. So, our team left to caucus about that offer. The vendors went to caucus about it as well. When they came back into the room, Marcus stood up and, after more insults, said, "All right, we'll take thirty cents on the dollar." I started to say, "It's a miracle . . ." but Syd looked at me and said, "Shut up."

On the drive home, I said, "Syd, how lucky were we?" He said, "I've never met such a naive young man. I've been working with Marcus for years. I called him Sunday night and told him to take the thirty percent. Those vendors had known you were going out of business. They have been overcharging you for the last ten months. They're doing just fine, trust me."

Highstoy was a public company, and the company eventually closed, so Syd's law firm packed up all the boxes of the material we had collected.

Even though we had closed, we were not done. We had one lawsuit from a shareholder. I called Syd and told him. He said, "No problem." I said, "We need the material that was in the boxes." And he said, "No problem." And I said, "Okay, please have their attorney call me." So, they called me, but nothing further happened with the lawsuit. I asked Syd, "Where does this lawsuit stand?"

He said, "Well, I took the boxes of all the records we collected, and I sent them to storage areas all over the United States, and I gave their lawyer these receipts as to where they were. They can go find them—or not." The issue went away.

Not long after, I was rehired by American Express and became the chief operating officer of their private banking group. I was once again welcomed back into the fold to create a business of client wealth with the bank. It was a nice transition back. Once again, I was in a job where I had no visible qualifications other than that people thought I'd done a good job before when I was there, and so they had brought me back. Some people were happy to see me, some were even more suspicious, and some ignored me. But I was much more confident about what I was doing, and so that's why I was recruited into the industry that Hank Greenberg had once scared me away from. The insurance business. It made the State Department look warm and welcoming. Once again, I was the new guy in an old place. And I was going to have to use all my wits to survive.

Chapter 8
"Never turn down a job not offered."

I got recruited to the Travelers Insurance Company in 1985 to start up an entirely new division for the business diversification group. Travelers was old, founded more than a century earlier in 1871. Not too long after, in 1897, Travelers was responsible for the first automobile policy and, in 1919, the first air travel policy and, by the late 1960s, the first space travel policy for the astronauts in the Apollo program. I was a senior vice president. I was now forty years old, and I made $165,000 a year, so I was earning four times my age and change.

This was a big new initiative for the chairman, Ed Budd. He was a lifer who had been in the job for twenty years and would stay around for another twenty. Jack Heilshorn had been recruited from Citibank to run this new initiative, and he was my boss. McKinsey, the famous consultant firm, had told them they needed to get around selling their products to their customers through agents. They needed to go to the customer directly.

To give you a sense of the state of things there, I spoke with my friend Hal Johnson, who was the guy who hired me for Travelers, and he can tell you why he did it. "I was the head of HR and the chief administrative officer for the company reporting to the CEO," recalled Hal Johnson. "Travelers' board had gone outside and decided the company should think about being something more than an insurance company, and so now they really wanted to be a diversified financial services company. I did the search for the candidate who would be the driver of this mission and, while the search firm presented us with several candidates, Chuck stood out. He had a very interesting background in terms of his being in government and then at Amex, so he made a lot of sense to us. He was really the guy who was going to drive the card business."

I was hired as senior vice president, and along with the title came the use of the corporate aircraft. I even had an office with my own bathroom. One of the things I found out was that it reminded me of the Oval Office, which also has its own bathroom. It seems grand to have your own bathroom but, the fact is, everybody knows what you're in there doing while they're waiting to speak to you. I much preferred to use the bathroom down the hall.

I believe that I was the youngest senior vice president in their history and the only one who had ever been hired from outside the walls. As a result of this precedent, the Travelers senior management did not accept me at all nor the program I was trying to implement. Once again, I was the FNG— the "fucking new guy." I was parked in isolation up in Hartford, Connecticut, on my own with no allies. It was like being back in the State Department—but worse.

I didn't like insurance. In trying to sell insurance directly to the Travelers clients, I was doing something that my colleagues all really hated because the company had used insurance agents for their entire history, and these people all had friends who were agents. I was barely tolerated. Going to work each day was hard and, in fact, one senior partner who was head of audit, I heard later, was secretly auditing my expenses, trying to catch me doing something criminal or immoral—or both. When they refused to put Jack Heilshorn on the board of directors, he quit. Now my lone ally was gone, and the wolves were circling.

"The CEO was a lifer with Travelers, an insurance guy through and through," Hal Johnson recalled. Hal had a lot of experience in human resource management, so his take on people was something that I took seriously. The CEO didn't have any appreciation or even understanding of the vision that Travelers was going to become a much more diversified company in financial services. We were making some real progress. "They introduced a card and started selling it, but the CEO was an insurance guy, and he just didn't get it. Insurance companies talk about being risk takers but, in fact, they're risk averse. They do everything they can to avoid taking risks," Hal Johnson recalled. "They charge you a lot of money to take the risks they do take, but they're incredibly careful, and so the traditional insurance guys really didn't want to do anything to upset the apple cart. So, guys like Chuck faced a lot of pressure from the traditional insurance people."

Travelers itself was under financial pressure. They were overextended in real estate as they tried to buy up Houston at a time when real estate prices there were spiraling downward. I saw the writing on the wall when they downsized the company, and I knew the end was nigh. We weren't relieved of our duties. We just didn't have a job anymore.

Through the executive search company, Russell

Reynolds, I went over to another credit card, Amex's competitor, Mastercard, to be head of customer relations—because I knew that I was better staying on the people side of a business equation. The problem with Mastercard was that they couldn't get the banks to sell Mastercard instead of Visa to the public. When I got there in 1989, Visa had a monopoly on the business. We had, as we would say, about nine percent of the "mail." It was so called because the Mastercard application for the card went out in the mail, and it was not coming back in the mail to us with business.

However, I kept working on it, so when I left we had shot up to forty-one percent of the mail. The main force behind this accomplishment was Keith Kendrick, head of marketing, who was brilliant in developing ads to enhance the brand. We worked together and became friends, but his ability played a great part in Mastercard's success.

Jerry McGrath was the head of recruiting, and he came on board at Mastercard a couple of years after I did. Jerry is a great guy and I liked him from the moment he joined. He has a great perspective on how we rolled at Mastercard.

"One of the first things I remember about Chuck is that I was two weeks into my job," Jerry recalled, "and you're always a little bit vulnerable and feeling like, 'Gee, how's this going to work out? And how am I doing?' At the time, my HR boss said, 'Hey, let's go see this guy, Chuck Wardell, upstairs.' So, we did. Chuck closed the door and started talking, authentically, about how he felt the place was being run and what he thought needed to be done. I could see my boss was squirming, but I remember thinking, 'Oh, man, this is great stuff, and I'm really comfortable with it.' Anyway, we're shaking hands at the end of the meeting, and Chuck said something to me that I'll never forget. He said, 'You know, you're doing really well here. People really like you.' And it was the first piece of feedback that anyone had given to me. Chuck also said, 'Okay, now that you're in the inner circle, you already have the seal of approval.' I just liked him, you know, from the very start. And I found him to be a fabulous leader."

I worked hard at Mastercard by expanding its brand and getting its name out there in more places and, while I got along with Jerry famously, the senior management team did not particularly appreciate me. In fact, my boss there, Peter Dempsey, was probably the worst boss I've ever had—but then, to him, I may have been the worst employee. I'm very straightforward, and he was anything but. He was British, and the most passive-aggressive human being I ever met.

"I knew Peter very well," Jerry McGrath recalled. "I became head of HR for the U.S. region, and Peter was the president of the U.S. region, so I became his HR officer. I was at all the Monday afternoon staff meetings with Chuck, which he hated. Sitting there for two hours just so Peter could go around the table and find out what everybody was doing. Peter was humorless, and Chuck is very funny, and they drove each other crazy because Peter wanted a compliant person who didn't have a lot of humanity and he just wanted to go over the weekly agenda, while Chuck was a much more freewheeling, unstructured, and spontaneous guy. Peter was not. Peter's schedule was the most important thing to him."

When I arrived at the company, Mastercard was the official card of Major League Baseball. I expanded the card into tennis and golf, two sports that have rocketed into the stratosphere in the past couple of decades.

I hired a consultant to put us into golf tournaments. I did it because I wanted a place to take clients from the banks, to get them to use the mail to sell us. It was a radical and different approach. Now, when you look at every big golf and tennis tournament throughout the world, you see the Mastercard logo. I started it, but if you went to Mastercard and told them this, they'd say, "Who the hell was he?"

"When Chuck signed on to Mastercard, which had recently rebranded itself from being called MasterCharge, it was really way, way behind Visa," McGrath recalled. "And Chuck really grew its share dramatically over the four years he was there by introducing this concept of co-branding. So, an alumni association of a university could have its own credit card. It would be co-branded with Mastercard and, thanks to Chuck, Mastercard was the first to permit that license."

Even so, with all my success there, I wasn't easy to manage. I never really fully embraced the great drama of corporate achievement. I cared about the money, but I was bored, and I was frustrated, and it showed when the two lines crossed. It was clear that my career at Mastercard was ending in the sense that I was never going to rise any higher there.

"He's a really interesting guy," McGrath said, "and he had a lot more going for him with his experience in life than Mastercard could capture or utilize."

In the end, Peter Dempsey fired almost everybody who worked for him. Including me. But Jerry McGrath did me a solid and, later, I would repay it.

When they let me go, Jerry was the guy who escorted me from the building, but he took me up the street to this beautiful office overlooking 6th Avenue and 57th Street that he had arranged for me to use. I saw that he had an envelope with him. I asked him what was inside. He said it was the terms of my severance. "It's X," he said. And I said, "Okay, I want one and a half times X." He said, "I'll see what I can do."

"And then, over the next two or three days, I went back trying to make appointments with people to sort it out," Jerry McGrath recalled. "I needed to get approval for this increased amount to pay Chuck, and no one would meet with me. I had told Chuck that we'd meet at that office on 57th Street again in a couple of days. And so, on the morning we were to meet, I just changed the initial amount on the letter to the amount he wanted, and then I signed it. I went to see him, and he looked at the envelope in my hand and he said, 'What's in there?' And I said, 'It's what you want.' He said, 'Okay, thank you very much.' We shook hands, and the next time I saw him was seven years later when he hired me to work at an executive search company in which Chuck was influential. So, he definitely paid me back, though that's not why I did what I did. He deserved it. And I was very happy to see him again and to work with him again." So, once Mastercard had cut me loose, I made a lateral move to the next ice flow when Citibank hired me to be a big part of Diners Club. It was 1993, and I relocated to Chicago where I did my best to organize and sell a product that soon dawned on me was one that not too many people wanted to buy.

Diners Club still exists, but it's not an independent card anymore. It's an affinity card that is part of Mastercard, which means it runs on the Mastercard railroad tracks and doing that solved Diners Club's acceptance problem. But when I was there it was a problem. No service establishment wanted to accept it. No diners wanted Diners Club.

During my time at Diners, I worked to try to get the product more widely accepted, but it was "tough sledding," as they say. One of the best things I got to do at Diners Club was to raise its profile, and I got to do that not in the office but on the golf course. I played golf with Jack Nicklaus, who had won 117 tournaments in his sixty-year career as a professional golfer, along with Cor Herkströter, the chairman and CEO of Shell, and Wendy's founder Dave Thomas. At Diners Club, we sponsored the inaugural Three Tour Golf Challenge, which was a golf tournament that ABC aired for one year, but I actually left Diners before it was broadcast. Even so, my connection to it got me a game with Jack Nicklaus.

Jack Nicklaus wasn't the easiest guy to play golf with as he was a pro, and everyone else was not. He was not in a good mood when we played, and he's a tough guy at the best of times. So, let's just say we did not linger on the 19th hole. Dave Thomas's firm had sponsored a TV golf tournament, so that's why he was there, and we became friends. I had met him previously when I was at Mastercard and had given him an entrepreneurial award. We talked about why the name of his company was Wendy's, and he said it was because that's how his daughter Melinda, who was the fourth of his five kids, pronounced her name: "Wendy."

He, too, served in the Army. We talked about how he learned to pressurize chicken and cook it faster and juicier under pressure when he was in the Army in Germany. This led him to start Kentucky Fried Chicken. He hired Colonel Sanders to market it. That was a stroke of genius as Colonel Sanders was, in reality, a state appointed colonel by the governor. He had no real military standing, but he has become a much-loved colonel eternally connected to fried chicken.

Eventually Thomas sold KFC to Pepsi and put that money into Wendy's, which made hamburgers fresh and square, not round and frozen, and that became one of the top fast-food outlets in the country. I didn't see him much toward the end of his life as he lived in Florida and died in 2002, at age 70, a bit before his time. Dave Thomas was fine as long as you were talking about Dave Thomas. I have to watch myself when it comes to that tendency because most people don't want to sit enraptured while someone else does all the talking. It's a problem I am trying to overcome, at times with minimal results.

While I did enjoy myself representing Diners Club on the golf links, it was the most discouraging year that

Come Up Big

I ever had spent in corporate America. While I was at Diners, I was pulled into a sexual harassment complaint by an employee who alleged impropriety. Her allegation was completely unfounded, and the courts threw it out, but it added to my Diners Club gloom. I thought to myself, "I'm getting up in the morning selling a product nobody wants, and I'm done." I was closing in on age fifty, so I was thinking that I was at the end of my corporate run. If you're not a genius in big corporate life, you don't get very far along into your fifties. And hundreds of people are on the ladder rungs behind you who want to climb into your desk and take over.

I had to take stock. I wasn't stranded in a jungle with no air support, and I wasn't knocking my head against college walls trying to get into the door, so things had been worse. I didn't have any puke strategy, either, nor did I have an MBA. So, I asked myself, "What are my skills?" which can be a depressing question to pose, particularly when you lack the skills that seem to be in demand.

I had come to value my role in the upper echelons of corporations and my ability to help people to succeed. They appreciated that, so I was well-connected. I knew how to assess people's strengths and, better still, their possibilities. I thought I'd be a great headhunter.

My friend Michael Brenner, who had done executive search work for me when I was at Mastercard, brought me into the executive search business. This took some courage because this move of mine was not universally accepted as a good idea. I remember John Johnson at the time, who was the chairman of the search firm, telling Mike to "get good, detailed references" about me. He needed evidence that I wasn't, as I had been called, "a cloud of hot air."

I passed, and so I got recruited to a headhunting firm called Lamalie, which was not well known in New York, but Lamalie was a big industrial firm out of Cleveland. It was at Lamalie that I learned to be a professional search executive. Most people just thought, "What happened to Chuck?"

When you joined the world of headhunting back in the 1990s, it was like burning your boats on the beach. You could not go back to corporate life once you had left to be a headhunter because, in leaving, you were seen to have abandoned the magical corporate path to their idea of success. At the time, joining an executive search firm was seen by many as a kind of surrender. If you could not do anything else, you became a headhunter. So my boats went up in flames, and I didn't look back.

I was the rookie, so once again the FNG. This was made apparent to me when I walked into my office at Lamalie—and there was water dripping on my desk from a leaking women's toilet above me and a dead rat under my desk. That was day one. Fortunately, from my perspective, I had seen much worse, and so I just got on with it.

It was at Lamalie that I met someone who became important to my work in the search industry, and that someone is Swami. Actually, her name is Liz Mercer, but I called her Swami for reasons that I will get into in a bit.

When I got to Lamalie, I was given an assistant who could not have cared less about being my assistant and, as I was learning about the business, this was far from ideal. So, the office manager asked Liz if she would help me out until they could find somebody. She said that she would until they found a permanent replacement, but she was so good and so pleasant to be around that I went to the office manager and said, "I want her full time." And that's how we started working together.

So, I had begun a new career strand, and I started to learn the intricate workings of executive search. Essentially, companies come to you with requests to find people to do a specific job, and you go out and find the right person to do that job. It's very niche.

I started to really understand the importance of the link between strategy and execution: you know what you aim to accomplish and then find the talent to do that. This was key in finding the right person at the right time with the right skills to do the job required.

I learned that I liked having an independent portfolio and of not being caught up in the corporate Kabuki dance of where your office was, how big it was, what your title was, and so on. My challenge was really my customers, not the firm. I learned that, through my background and my skills, I could reach a lot of people. I became quite good at the search business. And I came to love it. I was actually getting up in the morning and selling something that people wanted: the right leadership.

"Chuck also showed us all what kind of leader he was at Lamalie," Liz Mercer remembered. "There was a receptionist there. Her name was Mary, a lovely girl. Mary's husband worked on Wall Street and, when the market crashed, her husband was out of work. She was living life large on Long Island with a boat, cars, and a fancy home and, when all of this happened, they ended up losing everything. Mary wound up living in the basement in her mom's house with her two kids. Her husband ended up working with us, and he was doing little things in the mail room. I always talked to Mary, and she was upset one day. I asked her what was wrong. "Liz, I don't know how I'm going to pay the kids' tuition. We can't ask my parents."

"So, I happened to tell Chuck. He asked me to find out what school those kids went to. I did, and it was a Catholic school on Long Island. Chuck called the school and paid the tuition for those two kids who were just starting school until they finished the eighth grade. He's not going to tell you that. And nobody ever knew that he paid the tuition. I believe one of those kids ended up going to medical school. He made an investment in two good kids."

Well, I'm glad Swami included that story because I never would have told it—and that's because I had forgotten I had done this. Not because it wasn't an important thing to do, but I did it for that family, not for me. So, the point of the story is that you have to help the people around you because they are helping you.

Not too long after I landed Lamalie, I was next offered the job of president at a much smaller boutique search firm, one specializing in financial executive search. Word had spread that I was really not too bad at this search business, so I accepted, and I told Liz that I wanted to take her with me, but I couldn't take her right away. I asked her to give me time.

"Well, I was miserable without him, because the new boss that I had was, shall we say, horrible. So, I started looking for something else, and then I found something," Liz Mercer recalled. "And Chuck said, 'Please, don't do anything until I can get you here to meet the owner of the firm.' And he made that happen within two days."

Yes, that's true, but it seemed like the right thing to do, and so I did it. With Liz's help. And so, after I left Lamalie, I became president of Nordeman Grimm, which was a well-regarded New York City boutique firm specializing in executive services, and Liz came with me on that journey.

"That's really where the fun started," Liz remembers, "because it was a smaller firm, and it was just great." Among her many talents, Liz was also a palm reader, which is an art form I had not encountered before. "I don't want to brag, but I have a gift," Liz says.

"And so I would actually sit and read people's palms, but sometimes I would just get general feelings from people, and Chuck was very creeped out by it because a lot of the things that I would say were correct and would come true. So, he said, 'Oh, you're like a Swami.' And then he just started calling me Swami, but he referred to me as The Swam, right? So, I was like a noun."

And so, the fun began. Liz took full advantage of me when it came to playing practical jokes. Our office was right across from the St. Regis Hotel and in the afternoon, I would go to King Cole's bar with Maxfield

Parrish's big, lovely mural of King Cole hanging over the bottles lining the wall behind the bar for an iced tea and a cigar.

"Well, he was spending so much time there that I had the bartender's phone number, so I didn't have to walk over to go get him," Liz recalled. "He's over there having lunch. It's April Fool's Day. I'm like, 'What am I going to do to him?' I used to write a list for him every day: who called him from what phone number and what the message was. So, I put Mary Magdalene on his call list and just added a random phone number. And when he came back and was about to make his calls, he was so loud in his office with the door open, I could hear him reading off the list. And I hear 'Mary Magdalene, Mary Magdalene,' and he's saying it louder and louder.

And the girls in that office are hysterically laughing. Finally, Chuck yells out, 'Where do we know Mary Magdalene from?' and so I replied, 'The Bible,' and we all laughed, and then he slammed the door."

Sometimes Liz enjoyed her jokes more than I did. But once she got started, Liz was soon on a roll when it came to me and her jokes, which were always at my expense, and I would laugh eventually, as they were inspired.

"Once I phoned this toy store called Geppetto's in the Village, and I asked some random question, 'Oh, do you guys have a Fisher Price blah, blah, blah, and whatever?'" Liz remembered. "So, I found a toy store with good sales help. I wrote a phone message out and I put the name Ken Dahl, D-A-H-L at Geppetto's. Then, I wrote the phone number in the message. I also wrote

'Subject's looking for a CEO.' Chuck comes trotting in, and asks, 'Anybody looking for me?' I told him he had a message. A company needs a CEO. He went into his office, and everybody could hear him because the office is small, and he put his feet on the desk, the phone on speaker, and he dialed a number. And when they answered, he said, 'Chuck Wardell, here I'm looking for Ken Dahl.' And the kid working in the toy store said, 'Which one?' And Chuck said, 'You have more than one Ken Dahl?' And the kid said, 'We have Malibu Ken, pilot Ken, tanned Ken...' And Chuck said, 'Oh, my assistant thinks she's funny.' It was beautiful. It was just absolutely beautiful."

And so it was. I really enjoyed having these jokes played on me, and people could see that, and I was glad that Liz felt comfortable enough to do it. All of it gave me those qualities that I admired in leaders: of being approachable and of not taking yourself too seriously. When you do that, you can actually have some fun.

After four years at Nordeman Grimm, in August 2000, I went to Heidrick and Struggles, founded in 1953 in Chicago, and one of the country's oldest search companies, but the move came with complications. I was also being courted by the executive search firm Korn Ferry for a much bigger job and, if that worked out, then I was going to take it. So, there I was as the FNG at one executive search company and being hunted by another one. I told Heidrick about my situation, and they said that it was fine, that they wanted me for however long I could give them, so I worked from August to December, commuting to their Boston office from my home in New

York.

"I told Chuck that I didn't think I was coming with him if he went to Korn Ferry," Liz remembered. "And he said, 'Let's see what happens.'"

Liz also remembered the drama of the transition out. "So, we kept working at Heidrick and then, on a Sunday night, Chuck called me and said, 'When you get to work on Monday, pack the boxes. We're going to Korn Ferry.'" Liz did not want to go to Korn Ferry as she thought it was too big, so I had to create a plan to get her there.

"And you know," Liz laughs, "Chuck, being the very smart man that he is, got me this enormous pay raise, so he priced me out of the market. I couldn't leave him at that time because I was making much more than anyone else in my position so no one else would hire me. I had to go with him. And I did."

I'm glad to say that I was in a good position, too. Korn Ferry made me head of the eastern region. I was running their flagship New York office, which generated a great deal of their revenue. I started at Korn Ferry in 2001, and I stayed there until 2011, and, along the way, I had a very close look at high end corporate maneuvering.

I also got a close up look at 9/11. Our office was in midtown Manhattan in the MetLife building. Indeed, we had a bomb threat in our building on 9/11. I went back into our building while everyone else was pouring out. I wanted to make sure that no one was left behind. It was The Swam who said to me, "You're the only person I have met who doesn't mind dying."

Come Up Big

Liz Mercer recalled what happened after the 9/11 attacks. "Chuck called a meeting for the whole office, two hundred people. And he said, 'I just want you all to know that I know people have feelings about this. If you are afraid, if you are uncomfortable, if you feel any type of way, put your pencil down and go home, and we will not hold it against you. It's not a vacation day, and it's not a sick day. Just go and look after yourself.' Not a lot of people in his position were going to do that, and we were all so very grateful."

The troops were grateful but not so much the senior management. Paul Reilly was our CEO, and he did a nice job, but he left in the spring of 2006 to head Raymond James. Gary Burnison had joined the company the year after I did as the CFO. He was liked by the board and became, for the first time in my life, my much younger boss, sixteen years my junior. I was, at the time, about to turn sixty-one.

Burnison was based in California while I was in New York and, for reasons that have never quite been explained, Korn Ferry decided that I was no longer needed. I got called into a room at the Intercontinental Hotel in the middle of the afternoon.

In the room was the general counsel along with my boss, Bob Damon, who was hired over my head to run North America. I actually thought I had an opportunity to do that job, but I was told in April of that year that I wasn't picked. I remember saying to Paul Reilly, "There's a new Jewish holiday out there called Passed Over." On this day in the Intercontinental Hotel, Bob Damon, who was at the time the executive chairman of the Americas, never offered me a reasonable explanation of why I was being "fired." But ironically, I stayed put.

Interestingly, Bob departed from the firm in January 2015, under a very dark cloud, long after I had gone. Public information available about the issue is that Bob had been fired for defending women from abuse by CEO Burnison. Korn Ferry said it fired Bob for allegedly using his company email to solicit escorts and share photos of naked women.

In any case, they settled the Damon lawsuit in 2016, and Burnison is still the CEO.

I still feel very fond of the people at Korn Ferry, and the people who worked for me still remember me—for good reasons. The people who managed me didn't get my way of going about the job.

At this point, understandably enough, I thought I'd been fired. Not long after, though, I heard from Gary Burnison who now wanted me to get involved in "thought management." So, I put on a seminar at the elegant Links Club in New York City in December 2007 with remarkably interesting people in the audience.

The Links Club had been founded in 1917 by Charles Macdonald, a golf champion and founder of the United States Golf Association, as a place where powerful members of the golf world could keep the true spirit of the game alive off the golf course. By the time I was holding forth there, it had become, and remains, a favorite club for New York City CEOs, and that is to whom I was presenting ideas on thought management. So, from January onward through to April 1, I had the unique experience of working every day while I was being paid through my severance. The fact is, I was offered a very generous severance. And I never left.

"Oh, he most likely knew," Liz Mercer said. "The way Chuck always did things, any letter, anything he had assigned, was screened by his attorney, and with a fine-tooth comb. So, the way that Chuck had his offer letter written up, it was so much in his favor that they—Korn Ferry—didn't even realize what hit them. And he even put me in his letter. 'Should I choose to leave, Liz Mercer can come with me' because, sometimes, you can't poach people out. I think that, if they would have fired him, I believe he could have sued them for much more than what severance would have been."

In the end, I believe that Gary Burnison thought he had made a mistake.

Ironically, nobody in Korn Ferry knew what had happened. In November 2007, at a general meeting of staff, Gary Burnison had announced that I had come to them and asked to do something other than run the eastern region, and I got a standing ovation from the firm. They were happy that I would be back in the game.

In February of 2008, I was named one of the fifty best headhunters in the world by *Forbes* magazine. I won the Heidrick Award, which I think only two or three people at Korn Ferry had ever done, which is the Oscar of the search business. It is the highest award that the global executive search industry gives out. And yet, I was in this curious career bubble at Korn Ferry where I was there, but not really there.

Then I was asked to think about emerging markets, which was an odd request to someone who had been let go, sort of. I went to Bill King who has become a good friend and who was chief operating officer of North America and said, "You gotta make me an employee again, for Christ's sake!"

So, I went back on the payroll and back to the Korn Ferry world. I was now chairman of emerging markets and senior advisor to Gary who had fired me, but I had never left. It's a good lesson to keep your head high and your mouth shut, and eventually things might work out in your favor. Especially if you look like Michael Douglas. There is a story about that which The Swam can tell better than I can.

"Chuck was going to meet somebody for lunch," Liz recalled. "In the MetLife building where our offices were there was a restaurant called Tropica. He used to go there a lot for lunch because it was convenient. So, the guy that he's having lunch with calls me, and he said, 'Liz, I'm meeting Chuck at 12:30, and I don't know what he looks like.' I said, 'You know, I look at him every day, but I couldn't tell you what he looked like. He's about five-foot eight, but he likes to say 'six-foot-two, piercing green eyes, catlike movements, dark wavy hair, super-flex muscles.' But that's not Chuck. So, I said, 'Oh my god, this is embarrassing. I look at him every day, and I don't even know.' Then I said, 'He likes to think he looks like Michael Douglas.' After lunch, the guy called me and said, 'Liz, if you hadn't told me Michael Douglas, I wouldn't have met up with him. Michael Douglas is how I knew it was him.'"

Of course, Liz didn't stop there. I would meet people in the lobby of our building, and they would tell me that I looked like Michael Douglas. It became a thing everywhere I went.

"So now, he's really thinking he looks like Michael Douglas," Liz said. "And he was going for a teeth cleaning, so I got the dental hygienist to tell him he looked like Michael Douglas. So, he says to me, 'Even the hygienist thinks I look like him,' and that's when I had to come clean." I had a good laugh about that and quickly got used to the fact that I didn't look like Michael Douglas. The Swam knows very well that I look like Paul Newman.

So, while Liz kept things light, I kept slugging away. I was at a big turning point in my professional life. I was telling stories that were a hundred years old, and I could see the wave of talent who were twenty years younger than me becoming the next generation of leaders. I could see that, once again, the end was nigh.

Chapter 9
"All is lost, take to the boats!"

So at this point in my story, you might be wondering if I was sailing solo the entire time. No, I was not. I just didn't want to drag my family into the tale. Of course, you know about the family from which I came, but now I want to tell you about the year in which the world came crashing down around me, and some of that involved my family. I really thought that I would end 2010 living alone in a trailer in Florida bought for me by one of my brothers. I started to hand-wring in February of that year, and I didn't stop until September.

On February 1, my wife Kirstin moved out of our family home. We had met when we both worked at Mastercard, and we had been together since 1992. We married in 1996, and our daughter Andie was eight years old in 2010. I was sixty-four, and Kirstin was many years younger. She had told me a couple of months before her departure that she wanted to leave. I did not want a divorce, but in the end, that is what happened.

I had already been divorced. You might recall in Chapter 5 that I mentioned the young woman who was standing with me when I received my acceptance letter to Harvard. I also mentioned that I married her, which I did in June 1971. Cathie and I had a wedding for 140 people in Oyster Bay, NY. Then, Cathie moved to Harvard with me, and we lived off campus. I remember how happy I was with Cathie, who is a lovely lady. And we have two gorgeous children, Charlie and Diana, to whom I'm very close.

However, Cathie and I were divorced in 1982, and I pretty much figured that was it for me and marriage, until Kirstin and I tied the knot, and then I was once again a father a few years after the "ideal age for fathers" window had closed. Our daughter Andie was born in 2002. I was fifty-seven.

But I was delighted by Andie's arrival, and by our family life together, and Kirstin's announcement that she wanted a divorce was devastating. She also wanted me out of the house, but I said if she wanted to leave, she could leave, and I would stay here, taking care of Andie every two weeks, for two weeks at a time. That's what happened. Being with Andie, Charlie and Diana was a real pleasure in that terrible year.

Right after Kirstin departed, the IRS dropped a bomb on us. We were being audited, in a very detailed way, because they wanted to know why Kirstin had so many write-offs. She worked in TV, and she could write off a lot of her purchases for work, such as her clothes, her car, and even her makeup. But that is what had probably triggered the IRS. This IRS audit created a tremendous amount of work for us in dealing with our accountant as we responded to it. Fortunately we had kept our calendars up to date and we had kept our receipts, but we had a strong sense of pessimism when we sent our response into the IRS because we thought they would challenge everything.

Along with the complexities of my divorce and this forensic audit, I received a letter from the New York State Workers Compensation board opening an investigation against me. They informed me that I was being fined $15,000 and that there were some criminal aspects to the complaint because I did not have Workers Compensation for my nanny.

We had a wonderful nanny, Sarah, who looked after Andie and who has become a lifelong friend. New York State was coming after me, even though I had paid Sarah's taxes, to make her legal and to avoid paying her "off the books." My desire to pay her taxes had alerted New York State to her existence, and now they wanted to come after me for not having Workers Compensation in place. And so they did.

At the time, I also served on the Board of Directors for General Employment, a one-hundred-year-old staffing company based out of Chicago. In late March, the Board learned that there was a criminal investigation of the company by the FBI, the U.S. Attorney, and the New York State Banking authorities over a $2 million certificate of deposit that the new owner of General Employment had taken out of the Chase Bank and then had placed in the Park Avenue Bank, and which then seemed to have disappeared. General Employment was very much a public company and the authorities thought the Board may have orchestrated the disappearing millions. We were advised to hire criminal attorneys.

I went to see a criminal attorney about the matter, and he looked at me, as if sizing up an embezzler, and then said, "How much did you steal? I mean, I could probably get you out in six months, if you could pay it back." I was stunned.

The Board, so far as I knew, had not stolen anything from anyone, but three months into the year of

2010, things were looking pretty grim. Three strikes and you're out in baseball, but this was no game and there were more strikes to come.

In early April, the Hudson Valley Bank called my mortgage on the house in Armonk, New York, which was approximately $1,200,000. The Park Avenue Bank had failed, and the Hudson Valley Bank had taken over in receivership. My mortgage was current, and I had a perfect record of payment. It didn't matter to the Hudson Valley Bank. I obviously didn't have the money to pay it off, so they generously said that they would give me a few months until they foreclosed on me. In the meantime, my mortgage payments were going to be ten times more than I could afford starting on September 1. As we entered late April, my friend Dwight Miller died. Dwight and I had grown up in Cold Spring Harbor and we were close friends ever since our school days. He had gone to Yale, and then he was in the Navy during the Vietnam War. He returned to study law at the University of Virginia and then joined a well-known law firm, and he was the reason that I got a job at the American Express Company. He was a hockey player, a much better one than I was, and he was like a brother to me.

Dwight and his wife had taken a vacation to the Dominican Republic, and my friend died in his sleep. The Dominican authorities always investigate tourists who die there for evidence of foul play, and so they would not release his body until they had satisfied themselves that he had died a natural death.

His funeral was in Palm Beach, and of course, I went. Dwight was a big guy, and he was eventually cremated, so they put him into two cremation boxes and rolled him into the church the day before the funeral. He was almost late for his own funeral.

I came back to New York and put the Armonk house on the market, and I told Andie that we would find another place to live. Our old house was "modern," and out of style in the Armonk-Bedford area. There had been absolutely no interest from any buyer in our house, except for real estate agents telling my real estate agent that they thought the house wouldn't sell very quickly. Of course, this added to my real estate agent's natural pessimism about selling it at all.

By late spring, things were no better at work. I became kind of a Dead Man Walking at Korn Ferry as the replacement generation had taken over. I was aging out and I was already older than our new CEO by sixteen years. People were trying to be nice to me, but it was clear that my days were numbered. The ice was cracking all around me.

Not only that, but I was clearly losing my grip at work. Basically, I couldn't concentrate, because I was dealing with all of these other problems. However, I knew that if I left Korn Ferry I would be starting all over again at a place of mystery, and I really didn't have a lot of connections to start doing search work again. I and my wonderful assistant Deborah Crothers, who is also still a close friend, had been working together at Korn Ferry, and she was terrific. So, because she was with me, she came along when we were relegated to the office in Stamford Connecticut. She was also there when we were back in New York, but in a little satellite office across the street from HQ, an office which I named Elba.

We'd go to work in Elba, and Deb would sit behind my desk, and I'd sit opposite because I didn't know how to type, and I didn't want to answer the phone on my desk. "The calls would come in," Deborah Crothers recalled, "and I'd say, 'Just a moment, let me transfer you to the other phone.' Then I would transfer the call by handing Chuck the phone."

As for me, it turned out that I wasn't getting many calls because I wasn't doing much work in Elba, where there was just me and Deb Carothers and eight empty offices and a conference room. We had the run of the place, though. The code to enter the building was 1066—after the Battle of Hastings, which I thought appropriate because I was fighting a few battles that all added up to a very big one.

I was very distracted trying to do my work at Korn Ferry. On some days I headed downtown to see the criminal attorney, then the Workers Compensation attorney, and the accountant, and also the divorce attorney, and tried to find search work. The divorce wasn't going too well. It wasn't nasty, it was just increasingly more businesslike and a little more adversarial. I would go to see my lawyer Syd Platzer, who was my New York State Workers Compensation attorney, and also a good friend. I'll never forget when he said, "I hate seeing you all the time with your tail between your legs."

The first six months of 2010 was spent keeping the lawyers busy while I just kept trying to put one foot ahead of the other.

I had my daughter Andie staying with me for two weeks each month, and she would come to the office in Stamford and decorate the walls that I was climbing inside my head. I would go to her Parents Night at school, sit in the tiny chairs, and remain in a state of panic, more or less. She was in the second grade, and on one of those Parents Night visits they wanted the fathers to read aloud. I was afraid I was going to mess it up. As a dyslexic guy, I still get a cold sweat if somebody asks me to read aloud or to spell. They are not in my skill set.

Finally in June things started to change for the better. The IRS sent us a letter that said very kindly, "We accept your taxes as presented." So we were off the IRS hook. Then the New York State Workers Compensation case was also resolved in my favor. My attorney pointed out that our nanny Sarah had in fact worked less than forty hours a week, so her worker's comp was actually covered by my homeowners insurance. I got a letter saying that my $15,000 fine had now been reduced to zero.

But I still had the mortgage, the divorce and General Employment issue to deal with. I went to the bank and told them that I could not pay the crazy monthly mortgage payments but once I had sold the house I would then pay off the mortgage. They told me that they would work with me, and I often wondered what their idea of "working with me" was going to be.

It was now going into late June. We had a real estate open house so that real estate agents could come in and kick the tires. Nothing happened.

Then one day in early July, the real estate agent

called me up with good news. "Somebody and his father saw the house on video and want to come see it in person."

Their real estate agent informed mine that these two potential buyers had now looked at more than four hundred houses either in video or in person, and that they were "difficult people." She was sorry to bother us, but could she arrange a viewing? I was on the golf course when I got the call from my real estate agent, and I said, "Of course, but I have done nothing to make the house presentable." She signed off reassuringly, telling me, "It's just some guy and his father who want to see the house. Nothing's going to come of it."

So they did come to see it, and they stayed for four hours. They were New York City guys, who made kitchen cabinets downtown. I was asking $1.3 million and if I got it that would pay off the mortgage. Later, I got another call, and the agent said, "It's $75,000 less than you were asking, and it's his best and final offer." Best and final offer? It was the only offer on the house. Nobody else had even looked at it. I said, "I'll take it!"

The agent asked when I could leave, and I said I could be out that night if they let me stay in the garage. They did not make me do that, so I had a bit of time. During the summer, the house got inspected, and they discovered that the water in the well that came with the house had tested for three thousand times more lead than a human being could absorb. The actual cause was an electrical short in the water pump. There was also radon gas coming out of the rocks in the cellar that needed to be aerated. The swimming pool needed repair as tiles were missing; the fireplace needed work; and the front porch needed to be re-cemented. I said I would fix everything, and work was still underway when the buyer closed at the end of August. Nobody wanted him to close until the work was all done. His attorney certainly didn't. My attorney thought he never would. Everybody thought he was crazy. But he did close, and I fixed everything before he moved into the house in September. And of course, they could have strung out the closing until November, but had they done then I would have been facing a meeting with the Hudson Valley Bank that I did not want to go to. I mean, it was really tense.

But in the end, he bought that house, and I could pay off the mortgage. I'll never forget the day I went to the Hudson Valley Bank and said, "I've closed on my Armonk house and the mortgage has been settled." I was extremely proud to tell the banker that I had paid up. His response was, "Don't call me anymore. You're done, goodbye." The guy was all heart.

I wasn't quite done yet. There was still the criminal investigation into the $2 million that the Board had not stolen from General Employment. I had to go downtown to a meeting in the U.S. Attorney's office with my criminal attorney and I on one side, and the FBI and the New York banking criminal division and who knows who else on the other side. I had explained to them that we had given the money to the Park Avenue Bank as a certificate of deposit and believed it would be returned when asked.

Well, it turned out that the Board of Directors didn't steal General Employment's $2 million, but the guy who ran Park Avenue Bank stole it together with the new owner of General Employment. They both went to prison. When the SEC issued its report on the matter, they only ever referred to me as Audit Committee Member #2 because I had been innocent along with everybody else on the Board.

It had been a very long year, with the possibility of bankruptcy, prison, heavy government fines, all colored by the realities of divorce, along with single parenting, filling my days. That's why I was very glad to see the end of it. I was now sixty-five years old, and did not know what I was going to do next. But I was still here, and I took some consolation from the fact that the year that had just passed had not killed me. I had faced the issues, and I had overcome them. I had come to treasure my time as a single dad with all my children. My son Charlie made a huge effort to support his father along with Diana and Andie. It means the world to me. The divorce papers were finally signed in May 2011, the Armonk house mortgage was paid off, the Workers Compensation issue was found in error, the IRS matter was completely satisfied, and I still miss my friend Dwight Miller to this day.

Little did I know that after that year in which it all nearly fell apart, the following year would be one of the best in my life.

Chapter 10
"Praise the job gods."

Lo and behold, in the fall of 2010, I was at a cocktail party for the Association of American Search Consultants of which I was, at one point, the global chairman. Somebody whose son I had helped out many years before came up to me and said, "You know, you should run WittKieffer." They were a well-known search firm specializing in healthcare and education. I didn't even know that they were looking for a CEO. I said, "Look, I'm sixty-five years old, about to be sixty-six in April, and they're never going to hire me. They want someone twenty years younger." He said, "Well, I know the person doing the search work for the CEO, and I will call her and recommend you." And he did.

Janet Jones-Parker, the woman who was leading the WittKieffer search for a new boss, had called me and told a whopper. "Chuck, I have been saving you for last. You are the person to run WittKieffer. Would you come out and meet with the board?"

They sent me a very nice job description, which I thumbed through quickly after seeing that the job description said that they wanted somebody in their forties who was a management consultant, maybe somebody who had cut their teeth consulting for McKinsey. That was not me.

In January 2011, I was invited to Chicago because there were eight candidates left, and to my surprise, I was one of them. They started with 230 people when they began their search, but I also knew that, in this industry,

CEOs were almost always hired from within the company. Hiring one from the outside was rare, and WittKieffer was a well-known brand not looking to draw attention to itself by doing something radical. In other words, I wasn't expecting much.

Even so, I called a friend who was my chief financial officer at Korn Ferry, and she and I went out to lunch, and she ran me through the CEO interview drill. As I mentioned, I am not analytical or a numbers guy. I don't know why a balance sheet has to balance.

My friend said that my balance sheet quandary was something we could turn to advantage in my interview and then added some other things she thought the board might ask me, telling me to write it all down. I had a clipboard and wrote it all down. Then I flew out to Chicago, and now I was one of the final three candidates in April of 2011. Janet, who I thought had been kidding, had indeed arranged for me to be the last candidate interviewed by the board. Before that happened, however, I was interviewed on my own by Anna Phillips who was chair of the board at WittKieffer. She was the first person at WittKieffer to take stock of me, and she could have shown me the door. But she did not.

"We had interviewed a bunch of people, and Chuck was very countercultural for our firm," Anna Phillips recalled. "He was very unlike us. But he had experience. He had a certain level of confidence and experience in firms that were not unlike ours but, culturally, quite different. I was living my life in what I saw as a very purposeful way, trying to make a difference through this executive search in healthcare.

Chuck brought a business mind to the firm, and I realized that, after interviewing him alone, that I liked him right away, and I introduced him to the board." Before I went into the shootout with the entire board, Janet had told me that the board was very conservative, and that I was not to make any of my jokes, no matter what. I agreed to play it all straight down the line.

The two candidates who went into the room ahead of me were great. The first guy was from a large consulting firm. He was bright and used a PowerPoint presentation to lay out exactly how he was going to change the firm for the better. The second guy was an African American fellow and from another big search firm, who was also very bright and capable. And next, I walked in. Those two guys both had flashy prepared presentations to wow the board with facts and figures and data-data-data. I did not.

So when I walked in I saw that I was in a large Hollywood-type boardroom situated in the Trump Hotel in Chicago, overlooking the river. It was very much the kind of "Hey, I'm an insecure CEO" boardroom that you'd see on a reality show. It had large garish pictures hanging off the walls and the furniture was a touch too plush. I had both managed search work and done it, and I had done it pretty well, so I sat down at the end this boardroom's table and I started talking to them about how I ran a search firm. I began by saying, "You know, if you're going to have brain surgery, it's traditional to find somebody who's done it before."

These people were all consultants, and they looked at me in surprise. I went on, and said how I would go

Come Up Big

about running WittKieffer, and I referenced a line on their balance sheet, which of course they didn't have in front of them, but my lunch prep had set me up to deliver.

Even so, there was hostility in the room. They didn't want a New Yorker, and they didn't want somebody from a big firm, and they most certainly didn't want somebody who had worked in Washington for Nixon, because they hated him. There was one lady who didn't want a guy whose age she couldn't ask. By coincidence, it was April 27, which was my birthday. I consoled myself with the fact that at least until midnight tonight I was sixty-five years old. That seemed to me to be a great deal younger than sixty-six.

So, we started talking about how to develop a search firm. People were just staring back at me. Finally, this skeptical lady said, "Who'd you work for in Washington?" I had prepared for that question, and I said, "You know, it's increasingly awkward to talk knowingly about the Coolidge administration," which broke the room up as Calvin Coolidge had served from 1923 to 1929 as the thirtieth president of the United States. Which would have made me at least 111 years old, but it took my age off the table.

After I broke the "No jokes!" edict, we had a highly successful meeting. People started to ask me questions: what are the strategies? How do you market it? How do we grow from where we are? I answered them all, and I could see that they found my answers compelling. But, still, there were these two other fine candidates, both much younger than me and with much flashier presentations, so I said goodbye, and headed to

O'Hare Airport to fly back to New York.

I was at the Admirals Club at O'Hare, enjoying a birthday drink when I got the call saying that I was the chosen one. I was the new CEO of WittKieffer. In one of the nice congratulatory lies that are always told by search people to the chosen one, they said that picking me was totally unanimous, but I knew damn well that it hadn't been. The other thing looking me in the eye was now that I had unexpectedly won the job, I needed to extract myself from my erratic masters at Korn Ferry since WittKieffer was their direct competitor.

Now, when I left the hotel boardroom after the WittKieffer meeting, Janet Jones-Parker asked me if I had any conflicts or any "non-competes" or anything that could be an obstacle to them hiring me.

I said, "No, not at all." I was being honest when I said it because I had never really read the contract I had received from Korn Ferry, since that kind of endless legalese is impossible for me to digest. So, first, I went to see my attorney, Syd Platzer, who's a street-smart New York City guy used to finding workarounds, and he was adamant that I had none. He said, "There's no way you can go work for another company. You're absolutely locked in forever. You have to ask their permission, and they're not going to give it to you." So, I called Bill King who was, as I mentioned, an incredibly good friend and an honest broker. And he and Peter Dunn, who was then the general counsel, went to Gary Burnison and asked, "How do we release Chuck?" I was never one of Burnison's favorite people, but we had made our peace. Indeed, I was finally off the glide path of Gary saying,

Come Up Big

"Shoot the son of a bitch." So Burnison said, "Well, you have to give me something to work with and take to the board."

Bill King called me, and he said, sounding a little too happy, "We've worked this out. We will keep some of the money that we owe you. After all, Chuck, it is an elegant solution."

What they did was an elegant solution for them. They kept approximately a million dollars that they owed me that comprised my retirement benefits. So, once again, I was busted and disgusted, particularly as I was still going through an expensive divorce, but I was also taking a giant leap of faith that I could run a search firm in Chicago. I was also enormously delighted that I would finally get a chance to be CEO of a well-known firm. It was a happy birthday to me, specially so after the one in the almost-disaster year that was 2010.

I bought my way to higher ground, to put it in the language of the street. On June 15, 2011, I arrived in Oak Brook, Illinois to start my new job as CEO with WittKieffer, a firm that fired three out of its last four CEOs. I was going to be CEO number four. I was determined not to give them a 100 percent batting average.

Chapter 11
"Do it with the army you have."

The afternoon before I was to begin as the CEO of WittKieffer, I walked along the sidewalk in Oak Brook, Illinois from the Hilton Hotel, to get some air. There was a road with a big curve, and I saw a car come down the road and then fail to make the curve. The car drove up onto the grass, went crashing into the woods, and disappeared.

There was no one else around, and the first thing I thought was, "Did I really see that?" Then, because of my years of military training and so-called grace under pressure, I immediately called 411. Dyslexic moment. The operator told me I wanted 911, so I thanked her and called 911.

Eventually, the police came, and the police officer shouted at me because he couldn't see the car that I had called about and probably thought I was some delusional drunk. I told him the car he could not see had crashed into the woods, and so into the woods we went. I didn't know what we'd find on the other side. We approached the car and saw that the guy who had been driving it was now slumped over the wheel. He wasn't dead, but he had suffered from a diabetic coma. They flew a helicopter to the site and airlifted him to the hospital. Our timely arrival had saved his life.

They gave me the diabetic coma guy's name and home phone number, so I called his wife and introduced myself. I told her that I saw what happened and, if she ever needed a witness, I was the only one they needed because I was the only one who had seen it all. She was grateful to me and that he was alive, but I didn't hear from them again, so all, I trust, was well.

The next morning, I was about to start work at WittKieffer, this very conservative firm who had yet to learn that, when a new CEO starts, you send a car to pick him up. They did not do that, so I had to take the shuttle bus in from my hotel. As I was waiting for it in the lobby, the Muzak system was playing a song I knew and liked, called "Red Rubber Ball" by Paul Simon and Bruce Woodley, that had been a big hit for The Cyrkle in 1966. I still like the song a lot, and the chorus resonated profoundly with me as I waited for the bus. The words of the chorus told me that the worst was over and that it looked as if things were going to be all right, since the morning sun was shining as bright as a red rubber ball. After the events of 2010, this was truly music to my ears.

Then I rode the shuttle bus to my first day of work as the CEO.

I walked into the WittKieffer boardroom, which was much more modest than the garish thing in Chicago, as their "real" offices were comfortable but suburban. They had to swear me in before I became CEO, and I said to the troops that, before we began with the day's agenda, I wanted to tell them about something that had happened to me the night before.

"Last night," I said solemnly, "I became very well known to the Oak Brook police department."

It took a while for them to start laughing once they realized I was making a joke. I hadn't already been arrested for embezzlement, so we all had a good laugh.

With the tension broken, I told them the rest of the story. Then we all got down to it.

I was finally the boss, but the last thing I wanted was to play boss. As a result, I didn't do anything at all for my first ninety or so days, which attracted all kinds of negative attention. To those who didn't want to understand me, I was just sitting in my office, collecting a fat paycheck, and doing everything but working for the common good. Even so, I was working the whole time: I was watching the army perform and also learning all about WittKieffer.

"He didn't not do anything!" protests Anna Phillips. "He may think that, but he got to know everybody, and everybody got to know a little bit about him. He connected. And this was a huge contribution that he made. He really landed with the people who supported the consultants. He really connected with the assistants, with the clerks, with all the people who make things go in a firm like that, with the research people. There was hope that this was going to change on my part as there were a lot of people who were just pretty transactional with their support staff. And he really helped change that culture."

I was trying to learn how people in the firm went about treating its customers, and I could see that they were very scared. They were playing in a mid-level market, and the market was on its way to vanishing because of the consolidation of healthcare, a field in which WittKieffer specialized.

They had never played in the big time, and they were utterly terrified of playing on that field. They also did not like big time people. So, as I tried to think through the problem, I realized that this was not a firm that could aggressively go after its customers because they hadn't done so for fifty years. We had to build our way up slowly, by doing more for our existing customers and in doing so, to gain their confidence. Which, in turn, would give us a lot more confidence.

I wanted to slowly build the process of growing, not just through the marketplace, but organically and internally. I didn't want to bring in a bunch of outside hotshots. I wanted to fight with the army that I had.

However, the army was not yet completely on my side. Sally, who was our chief financial officer, was really rather doubtful of me. If she said the number was five, it was five. I could have said it was one hundred, and it could well have been one hundred, but nobody in the firm would have believed me. They would have believed her.

I'm sure it was "accidental" but, when I asked her to come to my office at 2 PM to discuss the business, she had the habit of never showing up. Her animosity towards me was real. I was someone from the outside intruding on her space, so I literally did that. I would just go down to her office and see her.

I had done a lot of search work when I was working at Nordeman Grimm and at Lamalie. I always wanted to be on the management side but, like most professional service firms, the management's side is always the weakest. I had to start doing search work to give myself the bona fides.

Now that I had them, I didn't do search work at

Korn Ferry because it was a big job to do what I was already doing there, and I didn't have the time to go headhunting. I also didn't do any search work at WittKieffer. I was the first CEO that they had ever employed who did not do search work. Everybody said, "How can we pay him if he doesn't do search work?" And as I said to the board, "I could never do enough search work personally to justify my existence, could I?" Their thinking was so ingrown. It wasn't until the last third of my tenure at WittKieffer that people saw our growth and our success and said, "Gee, this guy really knows what he's doing."

"Chuck would love to get the deal, close the deal, go in, get the business, and close it, and let other people do things in between." Liz Mercer said. "He was a dynamite manager and delegator. And he was very much a supporter of people who wanted to advance. So, if I ever wanted to advance, which I didn't, he would have supported it. If I needed to go to school, he would help. That's his nature."

My *modus operandi* was pretty simple. I would always find good people and then let them do the work you had hired them to do. I am fond of the expression, "Even if the mule is lame, it's better than carrying the wood yourself." So, I hired people who had much better skills than I did. They weren't lame at all, but you get the idea.

But in time, some of the most skeptical WittKieffer crowd said to me, "You're absolutely brilliant. You've opened our eyes." I'm not brilliant. I've never considered myself even close to brilliant but, thanks to my dyslexia,

I am pretty good at looking at the pieces of the mosaic and seeing how to align them and maximize them because it's the only skill I have—but it works. And, when necessary, I pitch in and get the job done.

Always—and especially when I was at the top—I was part of the team. I've always been hands-on. And my troops appreciated me, both in Vietnam and at WittKieffer. Over time, I began to win the WittKieffer trust. I wasn't going to blow the place up. I wasn't going to say that everything they had done so far was terrible and worthless, but I wanted to introduce new practices. And, as I said to them many times, "The buggy whip business is a great business until you sell your last buggy whip."

I really wanted to introduce them all to the idea of "Marketing Concepts." I wanted to promote division heads to give people a sense of possibility, and I generally wanted to get the firm out and into the world. I hired a PR firm to help with that, and there was great cane banging and harrumphing from the rear guard, but the board eventually came around.

In fact, I wanted to do more than just to introduce "Marketing Concepts" to the team. I very much wanted to greatly increase our marketing approach and to build an international practice, which we did in Edinburgh, and then in London.

I inherited a company that was pulling in about $31 million a year, and I wanted to grow bigger because I knew that we could, and I knew that we needed to do so to survive in the big leagues. I wanted to think about the business of search, and that's how I started every

WittKieffer meeting—by asking Sally the CFO, "Is the enterprise solvent?"

"We thought we were exceptional," Anna Phillips recalled about the corporate culture of WittKieffer when I joined. "And, in many ways, the firm is exceptional because a lot of people are mission driven. And we hired Chuck, a guy from Korn Ferry, who was from the dark side, and he was an outsider. He was an East Coaster. He brought, really, the first business perspective that we'd ever had. We all thought we knew something about business, but we didn't really know much. We knew about search. And so, immediately, he brought fresh ideas, and some of them got implemented, and he was able to help me realize some of my dreams for the firm and some of his own dreams and some other people's dreams."

Of course, amidst all of the good feeling that was developing, there were also many challenges and problems. Our business was shrinking because the small hospital market that we served was being absorbed by larger hospitals. We had to get into the bigger market to compete. And we were shrinking because of the attitude of the board.

This gem is a direct quote from the chairman of WittKieffer's board. "We hide our light under a bushel. We don't believe in marketing." The board, in those days, was composed of WittKieffer employees. I remember telling the board that they couldn't sell sex on a troop train, which as you can imagine in that buttoned-up Midwest world triggered the glaringly hostile stares that I was used to receiving. I wanted to do more for our existing clients and for everyone in the firm. So, Anna Phillips, the chair, and I eventually brought in three outside directors to quarterback the board. I wanted to open the musty windows in the court of WittKieffer to the world.

One of the things which was very important to me, because I hadn't had much of it in my own professional life, was being a boss who always presented the same face. You knew who you were dealing with when you came to work.

Every day, I told my jokes. I stumbled over words. My wonderful assistant, Val Fiedler, who is still with me, would say to people after I had mangled something, "I'll translate! I'll translate! I know what he meant to say." And so, she would translate me, and so she does to this day.

I wasn't interested, particularly, in the analytics of what we were doing, which are the numbers traveling on a "trend" basis. Numbers go where they go. I was interested in retaining people, creating revenue, and challenging the marketplace to accept a smaller company in their midst. So, when companies went looking to select one of the big four executive search firms, I wanted their people to say, "Yeah, we hired Witt not Korn Ferry," and everybody could see why.

I was able, as CEO, to extend a nurturing hand to people. For example, I had an assistant secretary named Kelly who was trying to raise kids on her own. There was a persistent car alarm going off in the parking lot, so I finally said to my assistant Val, "Who owns that car?" And she said, "Well, it's Kelly's. It's very old and has

300,000 miles on it." And I said, "Well, Kelly, why don't you get another car?" She said, "I can't afford the down payment," so I reached in my pocket and paid the down payment on a new car because, as I said, "You're driving your children as well as other people's children." So, she got herself a new used car, which led to her getting out of debt, which led to Section Eight housing, which led to her eventually becoming assistant to a major CEO in the Chicago area and getting a college education. But it was the beginning of the way up for her. Those are things that CEOs can do and should do.

I also liked other sayings such as "You get more flies with honey than you do with vinegar." But, also, the best companies succeed when they believe in the CEO. Their employees have to believe that they're not going to be chastised for making a mistake, and they understand that the quality of life is also part of why you work someplace. I put out an edict that said, "If your kids are playing soccer or if you have some important non-work-related event to go to, then please go to it." I wanted to make sure they knew that their lives beyond the office were valued by me.

Along the way, we had some interesting problems, one of which I'm particularly proud of fixing. Nine years before I arrived at WittKieffer, we were kicked out of the Texas Health Service System because one of our partners had placed the deputy to the CEO of Texas Health in a new job when the CEO had hired us to work for him to find a senior job for them. The CEO thought that was unethical, and he kicked us out. And he was right.

So, for the previous nine years, WittKieffer had

been speaking ill of the head of the Texas Health System, the biggest in the world, without coming to grips with the fact that maybe we should make amends.

Then came a stroke of luck. I learned that one of WittKieffer's recently arrived partners, Janet Abernathy, knew the CEO. I went to see her and suggested she "Go see him. Tell him there's a new sheriff in town who would like to fix this and do a search at any level for nothing because I think it's time that we acknowledge that we were wrong."

That offer was universally panned within the firm and within the board who resolutely told me that "We don't work for nothing." And I said, "Well, you're working for nothing now without the biggest healthcare system in the United States," which was also the biggest practice that we served. Or had served.

So, once again, I said, "We'll do it." Once again, the internal mechanism at WittKieffer said that we were never going to get the work. The internal thought was that it was not worth the travel cost to go pitch.

The unanimous senior response was that it was folly, and I was the fool. It reminded me of that old Wall Street expression, "If you're in a meeting and, after fifteen minutes, don't know who the schmuck is, then you're the schmuck." They thought I was the schmuck. But I was the boss. I persisted, so we went out and pitched Texas Health and Human Services.

And we won the job.

Now, the real hand wringing began, because I had said that we would do a search for nothing, and I meant it. I also said that whoever performed the work on this search, I would pay as if we were being paid for it. To the ingrown sense of the old ways of WittKieffer, that was outrageous. Number one, we were going to do it for nothing. And, number two, we were going to pay the partners who were doing it as if we'd been paid. It was a very high fee search. We weren't used to high fee searches when I got there, but we were when I left.

So, in what was a kind of grim, tight-lipped manner, a board member told me that while they approved of this, they didn't agree with it. They were going to sit back and watch me fail. So, with that inspiration in our back pocket, off we charged. We did the search, and we did a great job, and Texas was happy. The fee that I had passed on was about $700,000.

I got huge internal pressure to charge Texas Health for that money. I said, "No. You know, working for nothing means you're working for nothing." Now we did charge Texas Health for candidate interview expenses, but for WittKieffer work expenses I didn't charge anything at all. I let the troops know that we had all done a great job, and Texas Health acknowledged that we had all done a great job. The search was completed and closed in June. Texas said, "Thank you." I said, "You're welcome." And that was that.

Except it was not. Three months later, in September, to my pleasant surprise, the Texas Health System paid the $700,000 bill to WittKieffer. I never expected them to do that, but I got congratulations as if that had been my master plan all along. It wasn't. It was just a dividend from doing the right thing.

We've been doing work for Texas Health ever

since at a remarkably high level and as one of their favorite firms. That's the kind of entrepreneurial out-of-the-box thinking that I brought to the CEO world, and, in many ways, it represents how I looked at business. It was not understood by many as I was coming up, and I couldn't implement it until I became boss, but I did, and I succeeded because of it.

I also brought empathy to the role of CEO, something that I have learned is also part of dyslexia and which I'll take. Empathy is so absent in so many corporate environments where you are treated as a worker but not as a human being. I was told that a woman whom I had never met, but who worked for us, was dying of cancer. Her doctor had told her to go home and get her affairs in order because she had six months left on the planet.

Sally, the CFO, came into to my office and she said, "You know, we have this program that will pay her for disability for six weeks." I said, "No, we're going to pay her until she dies." Sally said, "Well, that sets a precedent, and we can't do that." But I replied, "I don't care about the precedent. If you get a letter from your doctor saying you're terminal, I will pay you till you die, period."

Well, we paid her until she died. At her memorial service, her husband got up and said, "I can't thank Chuck Wardell enough. You took care of our family."

And then all the families knew this. This precedent went all through the company and now people knew that, if life dealt you a blow, we would help you. I didn't do it for praise. I did it because, goddamn it, she had children.

It was the right thing to do. The precedent at WittKieffer still stands.

There were also perks to being CEO that, on paper, seemed to be high and mighty but, when you attended the event, they could provide unexpected amusement.

My friend Sir Richard Fursland, co-founder and CEO of British American Business, an influential transatlantic business organization, was asked by the British Embassy to host a lunch in New York for Prince Andrew who was serving as the UK trade envoy for the government's trade promotion arm, UK Trade & Investment. The point was for the prince to meet with about ten senior business executives invited to the occasion.

It was held at the U.S. Headquarters of HSBC, which stands for the Hong Kong and Shanghai Banking Corporation, though it is a British bank. It is one of the largest and wealthiest Europe-based banks with assets of around three trillion dollars. Richard would introduce the prince, and the HSBC CEO would moderate discussion after the prince's opening remarks. The pre-lunch drinks went smoothly, although the prince ruffled a few feathers by rather loudly disagreeing about U.S. real estate issues with a top executive of CBRE, the world's largest real estate firm.

In his introduction of the prince, Richard included two sentences of script provided by the British government, which said, "The prince has attended 150 occasions on behalf of U.K. Trade & Investment over the past year."

It was at this point that the prince, flushed of face,

loudly interrupted the gathering. He banged his knife on the table and he yelled at his private secretary who was seated at the foot of the table: "Why can you people never get this right? They [i.e., the staff at U.K. Trade & Investment] all work for me. I don't work for them."

The British consul-general did nothing to alleviate the awkwardness of the situation, so Richard broke the painful silence that followed by saying, "I stand—or rather I sit—corrected" and completed his introduction.

After Prince Andrew's lunchtime remarks, which mostly consisted of complaints about how he was treated by the British government, the HSBC CEO indicated most emphatically that, after seeing the prince's previous outburst, he wasn't going to moderate the discussion and risk exposing himself to a similar explosion, so Richard took back the reins.

After lunch, guests heard the prince thanking Richard for hosting the occasion—evidently completely unaware that he had hugely damaged the reputation of the British monarchy and, by extension, the U.K. as a country by his loud, irrational behavior in front of an influential group of mostly American business executives. For most of them, like me, it was our first encounter up close with this member of the British royal family.

Having enjoyed my lunch despite Andy's shenanigans, as I was leaving, I could not resist saying to Sir Richard the one thing that this lunch had made truly clear to me: "This guy was why we threw the tea in the harbor."

By the time that I left WittKieffer, I had made a lot

of really good friends who were now complimentary of my seven years at the helm. I had shown them an effective way to be a new old company. In my final year, they made me both chairman of the board and CEO, which was a great honor, especially considering their initial doubts about me. One of the things I'm very proud about is that, during my seven years at WittKieffer, not one senior partner left the company.

When it came time to say so long, the firm had grown to bringing in around $75 million in annual revenue, helped along by its international practice, its life science practice, and the others that we started that still exist and thrive. The firm continues to grow under the new CEO, Andrew Chastain, and today it earns about $125 million annually based on the foundation we built, plus Andrew has added an extra practice that handles temporary placement.

"Chuck helped the new CEO enormously," Anna Phillips said. "He made sure that he was doing everything he should do to make sure Andrew succeeded. He supported him and made sure that Andrew got a lot of mentors. Andrew would see Chuck as a mentor."

So, I ended my corporate career finally being able to be boss and finally being able to think out of the box, free to take the many risks that I took, and turning an old firm into a new one. I was leaving with everyone happy at what I had done and sorry to see me go. I figured that this had been my last job. I was wrong about that. I was just getting started on my next beginning.

Chapter 12
"Let my world take a look."

I really believe that I will hang up my skates, as the hockey expression has it, when I am around eighty-five years old. Then I will retire. That's because I am still too busy working—I am far from being done. I am the chairman of the board for three companies, and I recently "officially" retired as chairman of another one. I also have three wonderful children—Charlie, Diana, and Andie—and three grandchildren with whom I have great relationships. I'm not sitting back on the verandah sipping tea; I love to sail with my kids and grandkids, hang out with them and eat ice cream for dinner.

I have also reduced the stress in my life despite my continued commercial adventures and the fact that I am dealing with high-risk prostate cancer and, in fact, am a one hundred percent disabled Vietnam veteran. The way I look at my illness is that no one gets out of this life game alive, but cancer isn't going to be my ticket out. Indeed, after a long slog, I was recently declared NED: "No evidence of disease."

Even so, I still wrestle every day with being dyslexic and know that I always will. As a result, I still don't use a computer, though I have learned to become very handy with a cellphone. But this learning disability—or 'difference'—that had me counted out is something that I now take as a gift for seeing things differently: dyslexia lets me see and think outside the box, and more. It is a mysterious gift that keeps giving me challenges and insights in strange and wonderful ways, if I can understand it and use it wisely.

Mainly, though, I want to use my experience and my career to teach and inspire others to do some good in our world. One is helping Greenway, a commercial landscaping company out of Stamford, Connecticut, which devised a strategy of specializing in the construction and maintenance of grass fields for schools, towns, and cities. The second was to become the chairman of a boutique executive search firm, Heller, specializing in technology where I've been able to pass on the lessons that I have learned to a very able CEO named Martha Heller—even if I don't use a computer. And the third was getting involved in a publishing company called BookGo as I knew there were a lot of stories out there not being told, and I wanted to help create an easier path for writers to tell them.

My own story is pretty amazing, but it's all true. If you'd have told me at the beginning of my sentient life that I would be thought of as stupid, then get kicked out of Hamilton, then go to Vietnam, and next get into Harvard, then work in the White House and for the State Department, and following that inhabit the C-suite in some of the world's most illustrious companies, I might not have believed it. I still find it hard to believe.

I have led troops as well as a few workforces in two different centuries and have seen the face of the workforce change. I'm intrigued by this younger generation. I truly like them. I think that they're a very smart group and they're incredibly competitive. They're dealing on a world stage in a way that my generation certainly never had to do. I competed against Americans

Come Up Big

primarily for colleges and for jobs. However, my children are competing against the world for these posts. So, I am looking to help the younger generation as they make their way in our world. It's not easy.

I can be helpful in the next century. And, truly, I am not, at this stage of my life, trying to prove anything to anybody. I've enjoyed it, and I will continue to enjoy it. One of the things I find as I get older which is misleading is that age dampens drive, ambition, self, and satisfaction. I find it to be just the opposite. I find age a delightful challenge.

As I have said, I think sixty-five to eighty-five might be the most enjoyable twenty years of my life. I'm also looking way beyond that. I feel certain that I'll get into my nineties. I want, when it ends, for it will end, to have been able to develop a future for those who remain behind. Even at this stage of my life, I'm also increasingly grateful for and have a growing understanding of the people who built bridges. It's one thing I continue to try to do for others. Without certain people at a certain point, taking the time to write the letter or make the phone call, my career would have stalled out over and over again.

And that goes all the way back to being able to get a letter out of Hamilton—the place that asked me to leave—saying I was eligible for admission someplace else. Without that letter, things would have turned out differently. I can only imagine how.

My life today is wonderful. I can play golf when I want and travel when I want, and I can help people who need a leg up. Not necessarily in that order. I feel in good health despite the challenges which I have a handle on, and I have plans for the future. All told, it's not bad for an ex-hockey player who knows that you have to keep your head up when you have the puck—and your elbows up in the corners.

    I also know to be grateful to those who have helped you and then to pay it forward to help as many people as you can when you have the power to do so. Overall, my career worked. I always had an office with a door and that door was always open. Maybe best of all, I have received a paycheck every month for sixty years. And as my "helpful, thoughtful" brothers like to point out, "That's if you include Chuck's severance."

END

As unexpected as it is real: my Harvard diploma.

My red White House phone, linking my residence in Virginia directly to HQ.

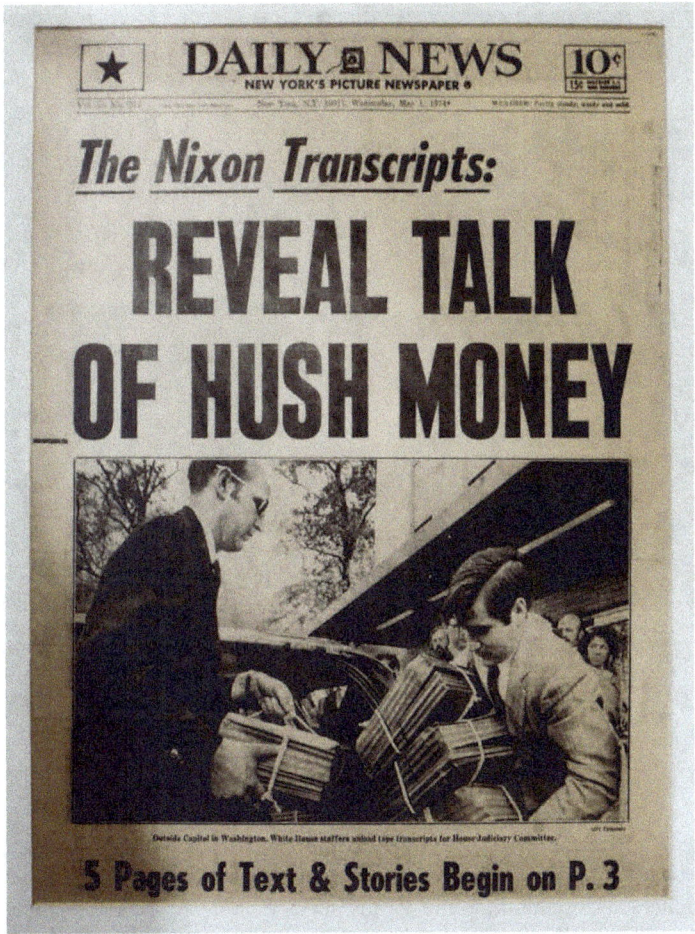

That's me taking the transcripts of the Nixon tapes to the House Judiciary Committee.

General Haig, thanking me for my service.

Charles W. B. Wardell III

May 15, 1973

Dear General Haig

    I am sorry to be late in writing to congratulate you on your new appointment. You have not spent many of the past few years in ordinary or conventional military positions, and this new assignment must be one of the most difficult and unorthodox. I am sure it has placed you in a more delicate and complicated situation than most people could realize, but I am also sure you are one of the few men that could step in at this point and pull the thing together -- and restore a measure of stability and common sense. The press seems to have lost its perspective entirely in this orgy of vindictiveness and recrimination.

    I am writing in part, General, to recommend a good friend of mine, Chuck Wardell -- who would very much like to work for you and whom I regard as one of the finest people I know.. He is graduating from Harvard this month with high academic honors and served in the Special Forces for several years before coming up to Harvard. He has the kind of absolute ability to get things done, and simple loyalty that military service develops, and if you need any additional staff for either the short term or longer, I think that Chuck would be extremely effective. I know he would regard it as a privilege to work for you, and I think that you would like him. I am taking the liberty of enclosing a resume and I am sure he could come down to talk with you if that would be useful.

    Although I am sure the relatively simpler job of running the Army was in many ways more gratifying to you personally, I have to say that I think your return to the President's Staff is a great stroke of good fortune for the country at a very difficult time.

This is my own copy of the letter David Halperin sent to General Haig. The letter changed my life, and gave me a life after Harvard.

President Nixon, thanking me for my service.

Charles W. B. Wardell III

> THE WHITE HOUSE
> WASHINGTON
>
> June 16, 1976
>
> Dear Chuck:
>
> I was sorry to learn that you are having to spend time in the hospital, but I was heartened by reports that you are doing fine following surgery and will be going home shortly.
>
> Mrs. Ford and I just want you to know that we are thinking of you as you recover. If the good wishes of your many friends can make you well, you should be back in stride in no time at all.
>
> Sincerely,
>
> Jerry Ford
>
> The Honorable Charles W. B. Wardell III
> George Washington University Hospital
> 2300 Pennsylvania Avenue, N.W.
> Washington, D. C. 20037

President Ford's message to me while I was in the hospital for an emergency appendix operation.

Come Up Big

When I left the White House for the Department of State, this was my parting gift from President Ford.

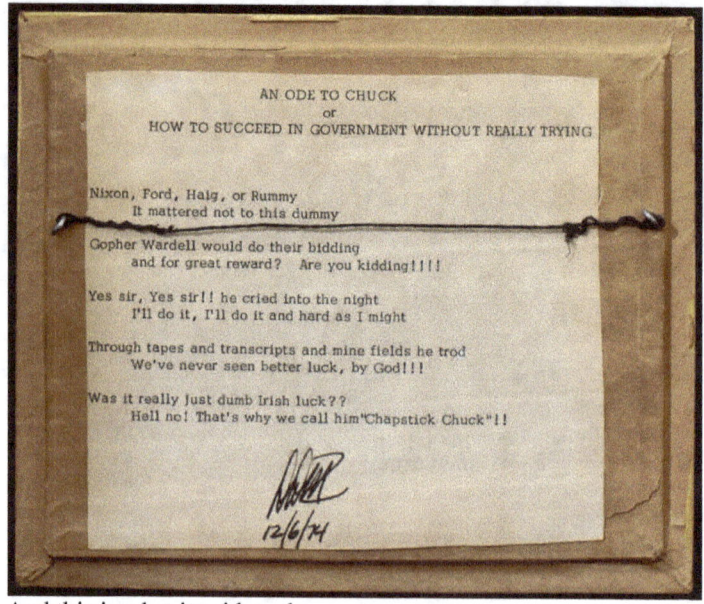

And this is what it said on the reverse.

Charles W. B. Wardell III

> **ADMIRAL ZUMWALT & ASSOCIATES, INC.**
> 1500 WILSON BOULEVARD, ARLINGTON, VIRGINIA 22209 (703)841-8960
>
> ELMO R. ZUMWALT, JR.
> PRESIDENT
>
> 12 September 1980
>
> Mr. James D. Robinson
> Chairman of the Board
> American Express Company
> American Express Plaza
> New York, New York 10004
>
> Dear Jim:
>
> Thank you for your letter of August 15.
>
> Now that our business matter has been successfully completed, I want to make a comment about Chuck Wardell.
>
> Chuck's strategy for the conduct of this negotiation, particularly his concept that the solution could never be found at the other end and had to be initiated from Washington, and the flawlessness with which he dealt with the various nuances, were noteworthy. My own willingness to take on this assignment was the result of my firsthand knowledge of Chuck's character and integrity.
>
> You have quite a remarkable person in this young man.
>
> Sincerely,
>
> Bud
>
> E. R. Zumwalt, Jr.
>
> bc. Chuck Wardell
>
> CORPORATE OFFICE: ROSSLYN CENTER 18th FLOOR   1700 N. MOORE STREET   ARLINGTON, VIRGINIA 22209

This is my own copy of the original letter from Admiral Zumwalt to Jim Robinson of Amex. I treasured the letter, fold marks and coffee stains and all. On some hard days, when I didn't know what the next day would bring, I'd look at it and damn well felt better about the future!

That's me, looking like a cast member of The Godfather, with my grandmother.

Secretary of State Kissinger's message to me. Note how he got my name wrong even here—"Jack" is corrected to "Chuck."

That's me at WittKieffer and Korn Ferry, trying to look like I know what I'm doing. Or "businesslike" as they say.

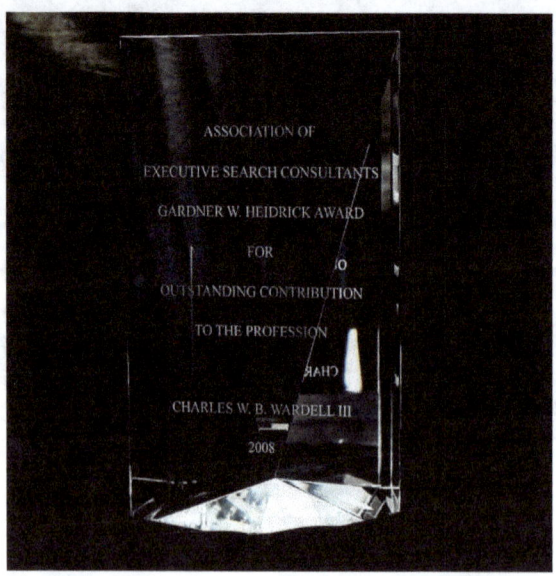

That's the Heidrick Award that I won in 2008, the Oscar of the executive search industry.

That's me banging the gong to say so long to cancer. As of June 2025, I am cancer free.

Come Up Big

Cheers to you all.

ACKNOWLEDGEMENTS

This book was written for my children, Charlie, Diana and Andie, who did not volunteer for the ride, but who made the journey so much better and still do. I also realize that the help I got on a day-to-day level from friends and my assistants along the way was absolutely invaluable, and so I wish to thank them for it.

I learned the importance of systems in the military, but I really learned the importance of an aide or an assistant in the White House. I realized that, when I went to work for General Haig, what the expectations were for an executive assistant.

I have also embraced the term "comrades in arms" as I've been blessed with many who worked with me. We've developed great lifelong friendships, beginning with the wonderful Muriel Hartley who was General Haig's secretary in the White House. When I got to American Express, I worked with Val La Sala, a wonderful lady from Queens whose first job out of Katie Gibbs, the secretarial school, was to be my assistant. We found our way through the labyrinth of the high end of American Express. She couldn't have been more helpful. She ended up marrying the CFO and having a delightful life.

When I started in executive search at Lamalie with Liz Mercer—who was affectionately known to me as "The Swami" because she really does see the future—she told me that I was going to be a parent again before I knew it myself, and she was right. One of her great lines—of many—was "Don't call me Italian. I'm Sicilian." We worked together for fourteen years. She overcame my handicap: she would type, and I would talk. I've never learned to use a computer. I still can't spell. Liz did both. We continue to be great friends.

After "The Swami" I worked with the wonderful Deborah Crothers who, during the hardest time of my life, when my marriage was ending and the wheels of fortune were definitely spinning against me, was always with me. We walked through very difficult times, and we remember. She, too, continues to be a dear friend.

Then there's Val Fiedler who has been my friend and assistant now going on fifteen years, and we continue to work together. Val has always been able to translate my sometimes dyslexic spoken words into understandable form. She still does.

I was extremely fortunate to work with a growing crew of people who cared about me. They had my back. I cared about them equally, and in our friendships, I realized how important it is to develop those kinds of contacts, relationships and loyalties because, in the end, you can't succeed without them.

And, of course, I cannot forget Shirley Prince who worked with me in Bahrain and gave me a few of my Chuckisms, my most frequent one being "put flowers around it" when you're delivering news that might need a little floral perfume. I don't need to put flowers around any of the people above. They are all my comrades in arms, and I could not have come up big without them.

I would like to thank my brothers and sister for their lifelong support and love. My sister Wendy has been my greatest fan from my Vietnam days and continues to support my effort that I made while I serving in the U.S. military. My brother David has always been a wise counselor, and I listen to him long and hard when I ask for advice. I would like to offer a special thanks to my brother Chris, who, when I began to make some money, was kind enough to spend eighteen months helping me find a way to keep a little of it, and through his wise counsel, I am now happily able to live a comfortable retirement.

Finally, I would like to thank Patricia G. Willmott, known as Patty, who I was lucky enough to meet seven years ago and who continues to be a wonderful friend, a great companion and who brings a great deal of serenity and joy to my life.

With thanks to them all, Chuck Wardell.

Index

A
Abernathy, Janet, 234
Adam, Elsa, 13
Air Force, 57,
Air Force One, 6–7, 133–35, 140, 162
Amazon, 150
American Express, 172–76, 178, 180–83, 186, 212
American Search Consultants, 219
Andie, 209–11, 213, 215, 218, 240, 257
Andrew, Prince, 237–38
Andrews Air Force Base, 7, 133
An Son Village, 73–74
Armored Cavalry Regiment, 48, 85
Armor School, 44–45
Armstrong, Neil, 136
Army Commendation Medal, 86, 105
Army Induction Center, Fort Hamilton, 37-38
Army of the Republic of Vietnam (ARVN), 58, 74, 76, 79–80, 84, 87
Army Transportation School, 98
Assistant Battalion Advisor, 74, 87
Association of American Search Consultants, 219

B
Bahrain, 180–81, 258
Bandar, Prince, 181–82
Baron, Renee, 34
Bay Ridge, 11, 90
Beliveau, Jean, 22
Binh Duong Province, 73–74
BookGo, 241
Brighton, 179–80
Bronze Star, 73–74, 101–102, 130, 155, 163, 171
Brook Club, 169
Brooklyn, 11–14, 37–39, 90
brother Chris, 15, 96, 108, 243, 259
brother David, 34, 96, 108, 243, 259
Buchanan, Patrick, 141

Buchanan, Shelly, 141
Burnison, Gary 204–6, 223–24
Bush, George W.,162
Buzhardt, Fred, 154

C
Calhoun, John C., 145
Campbell, John, 123, 130
Camp David, 153, 158
Captain Deere, 58, 66
Captain Moon, 51–52
Carter, Jimmy, 169–170
Cathie, 209–10
Cazenovia Junior College, 30–31
chairman, 8, 10, 131, 182–83, 187, 194, 196, 204, 207, 219, 231, 239, 240–41
Chapstick Chuck, 164
Charlie, 209-210, 218, 240, 257
Charlie Company, 124
Chastain, Andrew, 239
Cheney, Dick, 81, 161–63, 169
Chicago, 55, 194, 202, 211, 219–21, 224, 226
Chuckisms, 258
Churchill, Winston, 166–67
CIA, 166–67
Cold Spring Harbor, 12, 16, 25, 35, 38, 43, 60, 80, 92, 109, 130, 212; Beach Club at, 118
Cold War, 37, 155, 161
Colonel Leach, 79
Colonel Sanders, 195
Columbia University, 116–17, 131
Combat Infantry Badge, 73, 104
Communism, 37, 70–71, 77, 79, 82
Congress, 82, 148, 154
Coolidge, Calvin, 222
Cornell, 26–27
Cox, Archibald, 152
Crothers, Deborah, 213–14, 258

D
Damon, Bob, 204–5
Deke House, 25–26, 29
Dempsey, Peter, 191, 193
Diana, 210–11, 218, 240, 257
Diners Club, 175, 194–96

Dinh, Major, 59, 66–67, 101, 103
Distinguished Service Cross, 138
divorce, 209–10, 214–15, 218
Douglas, Michael, 207–8
Dryden, Ken, 27
Dunn, Peter, 223
duty, 61, 85, 87, 91, 125, 141–42, 177
dyslexia, 3, 9, 17–18, 23, 28–29, 38, 66, 142, 176, 215, 225, 229, 236, 240; International Dyslexia Association, 18

E

Eastern Hockey League, 34
East Woods Country Day, 16, 19, 33, 42, 92, 93
Eisenhower, Dwight, 1–2
El Toro, 7, 133

F

father, 1, 12, 14–16, 21–23, 30, 33, 36, 38, 43, 56, 91, 113–14, 131
Fairbank, John King, 128
FBI, 121, 133, 139, 141, 153, 211, 217
Fiedler, Val, 232, 258
First Oak Leaf Cluster, 74
FNG, 58, 60, 188, 197, 202
Ford, Gerald, 2, 160–64, 169, 250
Fort Bragg, 50
Fort Dix, 40
Fort Eustis, 41–44
Fort Hamilton, 37–40, 51; Induction Center for, 40
Fort Knox, 44–45
Fort Leonard Wood, 47–50
Fort Lewis, 41, 98
Fort Ord, 40
Frost, Robert, 63

G

Gadsby, Bill, 21
Geoffrion, Bernie, 22
General Creighton Abrams, 68
Gerstner, Lou, 176
Goldwater, Barry 158
Greenberg, Hank, 187
Gwin, Miss 133

H

Haig, Alexander 4, 6, 131, 133–43, 153–54, 157–59, 161, 163, 248–49, 259
Halperin, David, 131–34, 139, 154, 247
Hamburger Hill, 71–72, 111
Hamilton College, 10, 20, 22–33, 36, 110, 112, 115, 119, 126, 132, 135, 243–44; hockey team, 43
Harding, Warren G., 128
Hartley, Muriel, 136, 140, 159, 257
Harvard, 6, 10, 12, 116–30, 133–36, 141, 163, 171, 209, 241, 244, 247; business school test, 131
Heidrick and Struggles, 202–3,
Heidrick Award, 206, 254
Heilshorn, Jack, 187, 189
Heller, Martha, 241
Herkströter, Cor, 194
Highstoy, 184–85
Hitchman, Sergeant, 58–59, 65
hockey, 9, 16, 19–28, 31, 34, 42, 94, 97, 240, 243
Hoopes, David, 6, 142
Hotchkiss School, 20, 171
House Judiciary Committee, 245
House Select Committee on Foreign Aid, 149
Howe, Bradley, 116, 119
Howell, Harry, 21
HSBC, 237–38
Hudson Valley Bank, 212, 217

I

IQ test, 17, 39, 44
IRS, 210, 215, 218

J

Jackson, Andrew 145
Johnson, Hal, 187, 189
Johnson, Lyndon B., 37, 53, 82
Jones-Parker, Janet 219–223
Joulwan, George, 158

K

Kenyatta, Jomo, 166;
Kendrick, Keith, 191
Kennedy, Jackie, 144
Kennedy, John F., 128, 144–45
Kennedy, Robert, 55

Kennedy Special Warfare School, 50–51, 60, 130, 139; diploma from, 100
Kennedy, Ted, 71
Kenya, 166
King, Bill, 207, 223–24
King Jr., Martin Luther, 8, 54
Kirkland House, 122
Kirstin, 209–10
Kissinger, Henry, 132, 152, 161, 163, 168–69, 184
Korean War, 41, 63, 82, 137, 171
Korn Ferry, 202–7, 213–14, 220, 223, 229–33, 254
Kuwait City, 167

L

La Sala, Val, 257
Lake Forest College, 7, 36–37, 133
Lamalie, 197–200, 228, 257
Lam Son, 58, 80, 84
Laos, 51, 71, 84
Lincoln Sitting Room, 159
Links Club, 205
Long Island, 1, 12, 25, 30, 33, 35–36, 41, 43, 113–14, 123, 185, 199
Long Island Ducks, 20, 34
Louis, Jean, 34, 97
Luce, Henry, 14

M

Macdonald, Charles, 205
Madison Square Garden, 21
Manama, 180
Manhattan, 21, 34, 169, 184, 203
Mastercard, 190–96, 290
McGrath, Jerry, 190–93
McLean, Jack, 123–24, 126, 152–53
McLuckie Brown, Janet, 179
Mekong Delta, 44
Mercer, Liz, 197–201, 205, 206, 229, 257; as Swami, 197, 199–200, 257–58
Messina, Sal, 20–21
Meyer, Arnold Luther, 13
Meyer, Caroline, 13
Meyer, Ida Helen Kusenberg, 13
Middle East, 180–81, 184
Military Assistance Command Vietnam, 57, 68
Miller, Brad, 34
Miller, Dwight, 20, 23, 95, 109, 171, 212, 218
Moon, Walter Hugh, 51
mother, 13–15, 33, 38–39, 48, 56, 70, 90, 108, 114–15
Moynihan, Daniel, 128–29, 136, 139, 141

N

National Hockey League (NHL), 20–21, 27, 34
National Security Council, 122
Navy, 12, 38, 41, 45, 109, 132, 154–56, 162, 166, 181, 213
New Jersey, 11, 13, 40, 65
Newman, Paul, 209
New York, 1, 20, 24, 34, 56, 60, 108, 174, 181, 212–17, 238
New York Daily News, 157, 164
New York State Workers Compensation, 210–11, 214–15
New York Times, 35
Nicklaus, Jack, 195
Nixon, Richard, 2, 4, 6–7, 71, 83, 136, 140, 144–49, 152–54, 157–64, 222, 248; resignation of, 161
Nordeman Grimm, 200, 202, 228
North Vietnam, 37, 151
North Vietnamese, 52, 59, 62, 65, 69, 71, 76–78, 82–84, 86, 136, 151

O

Oakland Army Terminal, 56, 108
O'Brien, Jerry, 23
Officers' Candidate School (OCS), 44–47
Oval Office, 143, 147, 157, 160, 188
Owl Club, 123–26, 130

P

parents, 12–15, 19–20, 24, 28, 44, 63, 107, 112, 129, 199, 215
Park Avenue Bank, 211–12, 217–18
Parker, David, 149

Patton IV, Colonel George S., 70, 85
People's Army of Vietnam (PAVN), 65, 71
Phillips, Anna, 220, 227, 231–32
Pinochet, Augusto, 151
Platzer, Syd, 184, 214, 2243
Prentice, Dean, 21
presidents, 1–2, 4, 6–7, 54–55, 135–36, 138–44, 147–50, 158–60, 167, 183, 200–201
Price, Ray, 160
Prince, Shirley, 258
PTSD, 32, 109–10, 124

R

Rangers, 20–22
Reilly, Paul, 205
Richard, Maurice "The Rocket," 22
Robinson, James Dixon III, 172–73, 178–79, 182, 251
Roosevelt, Theodore, 1–2
Rorschach test, 120
Rumsfeld, Donald, 161–63, 169

S

Sagamore Hill, 1–2
Saigon, 57, 65, 108
Sally, 228, 231, 236
San Clemente, 6–7, 136, 140–42, 161
Saudi Arabia, 180–82
Scowcroft, Brent, 136
Seaman, Barry, 25, 28–30
search business, 196, 198–199, 206
Shannon, Ryan, 20
Simon, Paul, 226
South Korea, 165–66
South Vietnam, 37, 52–53, 58–59, 66, 72, 77–78, 81–83, 151–52
Spears, Sergeant James 71
Spiro, Agnew, 145–46
Stanley Cup, 22, 27
State Department, 3, 8, 10, 163, 165–68, 171–73, 177, 186, 188, 241, 250

T

Taft, 18–20, 22–25, 28, 64, 94, 114–16, 130, 177
Teller, Edward, 184
Tennyson, Alfred Lord, 169
Tet Offensive, 53–54, 84
Texas Health, 233–35
Thatcher, Margaret, 169, 179
Thomas, Dave, 194
Thomas, Norman, 35–36, 133
Tolls, Dean, 9
Tour Golf Challenge, 195
Travelers Insurance Company, 187

U

UK Trade & Investment, 237
Ullman, Liv, 136
United States Army, 32, 47, 56, 75, 85–88; advisory group of, 87; infantry division of, 50, 74; instructors in, 41–42
United States Golf Association, 205

V

Viet Cong, 52–53, 59, 65, 70, 72
Vietnam, 32–33, 37–38, 40–41, 44–51, 53–58, 60–61, 64–65, 67–72, 76, 78, 80–83, 85–88, 106–14, 119–22, 124–25, 129–31, 137–39, 156, 172–73; draft, 32
Vietnamese Medal of Honor, 73

W

Wardell, Elmore, 12
Wardell, Jacob, 11
Wardell, Margaret Adelia, 11–12
Wardell, Thomas, 10
Wardell, Winant Bennett, 11–12
Wardells, 10–12, 14, 39, 48, 74, 133, 176, 178
Wardell's Corner, 11
Wardellville, 11
Washington, D.C., 7, 25, 29, 31, 132–33, 138, 147, 154–58, 169, 182–83, 222
Watergate, 8, 131, 135, 137–39, 144–45, 149–52, 154, 157, 161, 168, 172
Waters, George, 172–74, 176, 179–80
Wells, Sergeant, 50
Wendy, 15, 56, 96, 258
White House, 1–4, 6–7, 10, 25, 29,

31, 131–54, 157–64, 169, 172, 176–78, 241, 244, 250, 257
White, Teddy, 122, 143–44
Willard, Charles, 11
Willmott, Patricia G., 259
Winter Club, 16, 19
WittKieffer, 149, 220–239
Woodley, Bruce, 226
Woods, Rose Mary, 149
World War I, 50, 78
World War II, 12, 19, 38, 60, 70, 78, 80–82, 85, 91, 111–12, 121, 123, 156
Worsley, Lorne 21

Z

Zaire, 167
Zhou Enlai, 144
Zumwalt, Admiral Elmo, 132, 154–55, 157, 171, 181–83, 251

www.ingramcontent.com/pod-product-compliance
Lightning Source LLC
Chambersburg PA
CBHW050526100526
44581CB00008B/147/J